# THE
# AFTER WORK
## COOKBOOK

*Kirsten Tilgals & Nicole Gaunt*

Crescent Books
New York • Avenel

# Contents

The recipes in this book are not meant to be followed to the letter. Rather, they should provide ideas and guidance for when you often feel the least inspired – after work. They are based on the idea of minimum effort, and take into account that most of us don't have a kitchen full of fresh produce because we haven't had time to shop for a week.

It is possible to make appealing meals from a few items in your cupboards, supplemented with a few things from the local store or deli. The first step to eating well is shopping well. Rather than just frozen TV-dinners, you need to stock your kitchen with staples. These will form the basis of many interesting meals when added to a minimal amount of readily-available fresh ingredients.

## Pasta

Although fresh pasta is now commonly available, it only keeps for a few days in the refrigerator whereas dried pasta keeps almost indefinitely.

### TO COOK PERFECT PASTA

1. Use lots and lots of water so that the pasta can move around.
   Bring to a rapid boil and keep boiling, even when adding pasta.
   Add a dash of olive oil and a pinch of salt.
2. Add all the pasta at once, stir to ensure none of it is sticking together, and continue to stir regularly through out cooking.
3. Do not overcook. Check the pasta a few minutes before you think it will be done and keep checking until it is al dente (meaning it offers only just a little resistance when bitten).
4. Drain quickly in a colander and run a little water through.
   Serve immediately.

Cooking time depends on the shape and size of the pasta. If you can't serve it straight away, toss with a little olive oil to keep moist. You should do this if you are storing leftover pasta too. If you need to keep the pasta warm, return it to the dry but warm pan and cover. To reheat already-cooked pasta, add it to freshly boiling water for about 30 seconds.

## Rice

There is a variety of white rice available, including long-grain, short-grain, and arborio rice (see page 28), and perfumed long-grain rices such as basmati and jasmine. There is also wild rice which is not a rice at all, but a kind of aquatic sea grass. Store white rice in a sealed container in a cool, dark place; it will keep for over a year. Brown rice will keep for a few months if stored in the refrigerator.

### COOKING GREAT RICE

Most rice can be cooked using the absorption method. For each cup of rice, use the indicated amount of water: medium to long-grain rice — $1\frac{3}{4}$-2 cups, short-grain rice — $1\frac{1}{2}$-2 cups, basmati — $1\frac{1}{2}$ cups.

First, rinse rice well. Place in a saucepan with water and bring mixture to the boil over high heat. Stir once, cover tightly, and reduce heat to low. Cook according to the time indicated on the packet, usually 15 to 20 minutes, without lifting lid. If all water has not been absorbed, cover again and cook for a few more minutes. When done, fluff rice with a fork and let stand covered for a few minutes off the heat.

Leftover rice will keep for about 1 week in the refrigerator. Reheat by sprinkling with water, and placing in the microwave or in a covered saucepan over low heat for a few minutes.

Try cooking rice in stock or adding herbs to the cooking water for added flavor.

## Couscous

Although often used as an alternative to rice, couscous is actually tiny rolled beads of semolina flour. It could be the perfect afterwork ingredient as it only requires a few minutes soaking before eating (see page 30) and will keep almost indefinitely in a sealed container in a dark, dry place.

## Potatoes

Potatoes should never be undervalued. They're hardy, long-lasting and don't involve any fuss when cooking. Choose them washed if you prefer but keep in mind that they keep longer if dirt-covered and stored in a dark place.

The humble potato can be transformed into a wide range of dishes from the warm comfort of mashed potatoes to crispy, bold potato wedges. Some types, however, are better suited than others to their final incarnation. Use this guide as a start:
- baby or new potatoes — these are best boiled and served as a side dish or in potato salads (with the skins on). They can also be baked.
- old and floury or mealy potatoes — these are large and usually covered in dirt when you buy them. They are best for baking in their skins or for boiling and mashing.
- slightly yellow or white-fleshed waxy potatoes — these are best peeled and then roasted, baked as wedges, or fried.
- very waxy potatoes are suited to salads.

**TO MAKE CLASSIC MASHED POTATO**

Peel and cut big floury potatoes in quarters and place in cold salted water to cover. Bring to the boil and cook covered until tender, about 20-30 minutes. Test with a skewer. Drain, then return to hot saucepan and leave for a couple of minutes until extra moisture evaporates, shaking occasionally. Add hot milk, butter, salt, and pepper and mash with a fork until smooth. If you like your potatoes extra creamy, beat with a wooden spoon.

Try adding a finely chopped white onion or scallion and a chopped garlic clove while mashing. Or add grated gruyere or cheddar cheese. Be really decadent and use hot bacon fat instead of butter when mashing!

Pulses is the general name for dried beans, peas, and lentils. They make a great basis for a meal as they are inexpensive, simple to prepare, very filling, and high in protein. Some of the most popular are:

- haricot or white beans — these include navy beans, soissons, and flageolets
- cannellini beans
- butter or lima beans
- borlotti beans
- chick peas, ceci peas, or garbanzo beans
- red kidney beans
- broad or fava beans
- black-eyed beans or peas

You can store dried pulses, tightly sealed, in a dark, dry place for up to 1 year. You can also buy most pulses already prepared and canned which cuts time and effort considerably.

**TO COOK DRIED BEANS**

First, rinse thoroughly and sort out any undesirable pieces. Cover with water and soak for several hours or overnight. Rinse, then cover with fresh water in a saucepan and simmer until tender. You can add garlic, bay leaves, chili, or other spices but don't add salt, sugar, or acids (such as tomatoes) until after cooking as this can toughen the beans.

Dried lentils need no presoaking, and small red lentils only take about 15 minutes to cook. Brown and green lentils take a little longer. Place in a saucepan with enough cold water to cover. Bring to the boil then simmer until just tender, not mushy.

## Chili beans

A 14 oz (400 g) can of kidney beans, drained, is a versatile ingredient in afterwork eating. Transformed into basic chili beans, you can then serve in a variety of ways.

Try cooking onions in a little oil in a small pan until soft. Add kidney beans, a drained can of peeled tomatoes, and hot chili sauce to taste and simmer gently for 10 minutes. Pile onto corn tortilla chips, serve with sour cream and avocado, and you have nachos. Blend in a food processor and you have a spicy dip. You can also try adding a little turmeric, oregano, cumin, and cayenne pepper.

For more of a meal, don't drain the tomatoes, and add a small can of corn and some chopped green pepper (capsicum). Just heat through and serve with steamed rice, topped with grated cheese. Or spoon the mixture into taco shells along with shredded lettuce and grated cheese.

*Opposite: Tuna and Beans (see page 66)*

| Nuts and seeds | Buy nuts in their shells if possible as they keep far longer. Once shelled, they are best kept in a sealed container in the refrigerator or freezer. Otherwise, store in a cool, dry place. The same applies to seeds. |

**TOASTING** Both nuts and seeds taste even better when toasted. Spread them evenly over a flat tray under the broiler (grill) or in a hot oven, or in a dry heavy-based frying pan over medium-high heat, and cook until golden. Shake pan occasionally to ensure even toasting. Keep watch as they start browning slowly and then seem to burn before you know it.

*Herbs and spices*

To store fresh herbs, wash and dry carefully (a salad spinner works well). Store in a sealed plastic container in refrigerator for about 1 week or more. Herbs with a fair amount of moisture in the leaves (such as mint or basil) can be chopped, mixed with a spoonful of water and frozen in ice cube trays; just pop a frozen cube straight into a dish when cooking. Better yet, grow herbs by a window or in the garden so that you always have some to hand — wipe them with a damp cloth before using.

In the same way, your own lemon tree and chili plant will help you out of many culinary corners. However, really fresh lemons will keep for months in the refrigerator (if they haven't already been in cold-storage). Chilies can be purchased dried, but jars of minced chili are handiest for the afterwork cook. The Asian version known as sambal olek is recommended.

Dried herbs should be kept in a dry, dark place. Ground seasonings lose their potency quicker, so invest in a mortar and pestle and buy whole when possible. As a rule, use half as much dried herb as you would fresh.

**CURRY** What we refer to as curry is not just curry leaves but a blend of different spices. Curry powders and pastes vary hugely so experiment and find a few that suit your tastes. Most contain cumin, turmeric, and coriander among other spices. Note that ground coriander is made from the seeds of the plant and is very different from the fresh leaves, which are also known as cilantro.

## Thai green or red curry

Thai-style curry is very different from Indian dishes. To make a basic green or red curry: heat a spoonful of oil in a wok and stir-fry 1 lb (500 g) beef or chicken strips or an assortment of vegetables (onion segments, broccoli, red pepper strips, slices of zucchini/courgettes, snow peas/mange tout, green beans). Add a couple of spoonsful of curry paste and fry for a minute until aromatic. Add a cup or two of coconut milk and simmer for 10 minutes. Serve with steamed rice.

## Roasted garlic

You won't believe it until you try it but roasted whole cloves of garlic are just sublime (and not at all overpowering). They make a wonderful accompaniment to roasted meats and vegetables. Toss the soft cloves through hot pasta with black pepper and olive oil. Or spread the warm garlic onto good bread or pizza base and eat it alone or with tomato and sardines.

Preheat oven to 350°F (180°C/Gas 4). Cut the top of whole unpeeled heads (that is, the cluster of cloves) to reveal the tops of the cloves. Drizzle a little olive oil over and bake about 30-45 minutes until garlic is really soft and oozing. To eat, squeeze out the garlic from the casing.

### GARLIC

Store in a dry, airy place. Before purchase, check that the cloves are not already dry and shrivelling in the skin. To peel, push down on a clove of garlic with the flat side of a knife. This not only "bruises" the garlic, releasing its aromatic juices, but splits the skin for easy removal.

### GINGER

Store in a cool, dry place. When ready to use, peel off the outside of the root with a small knife. If it is starting to dry up, peel as well as you can and then grate finely. Ginger can also be bought already minced in jars.

### SALT AND PEPPER

Freshly ground black pepper can lift any dish out of the doldrums; stock whole black peppercorns and grind only when needed in a pepper grinder. Invest in sea salt flakes as well for extra taste.

### Dried mushrooms

Dried mushrooms have a wonderful robust flavor. The Japanese shiitake and the Italian porcini mushrooms (cepes) are both readily available, and can be stored for years in a sealed container in a dark, dry place.

#### TO PREPARE

Soak them in hot water for 20-30 minutes before use, then remove, rinse carefully and dry on paper towels. The soaking liquid can be used in a recipe or as a stock in a soup or sauce. Ideally, it should be strained through fine cloth such as cheesecloth or muslin, or through coffee filter paper, before use.

### Sauces and condiments

Tomato paste is an essential ingredient in many recipes but it tends to grow mold quickly. To avoid this, purchase in single-use packs or store a jar, once opened, upside-down in the refrigerator.

As well as peeled tomatoes, it is worthwhile keeping a jar or can of passata. This is made from tomatoes that are chopped and not quite pureed; useful for an instant sauce.

Tapenade is a paste made from olives, very popular in Mediterranean cooking. Try some dobbed on baked potatoes, toss a big spoonful through a bowl of hot pasta, or spread generously on fresh crusty bread and top with a slice of ripe red tomato and a mild cheese such as bocconcini or mozzarella.

You can keep whole olives that have been cured in oil or brine in jars in the cupboard for years. They'll last for months in the refrigerator after opening; if a white film develops, just rinse as it indicates crystallized salt, not spoilage (spoiled olives go very soft).

Tahini is a middle eastern ingredient that has been steadily growing in popularity due to its great nutty taste and high nutritional value. A sesame seed paste, this protein-rich food can be found in supermarkets, delis, and health food stores. Unopened jars will keep for up to a year, although the oil may separate from the paste and need mixing before use. Try it thinned with lemon juice and cold water as a salad dressing, spread on a whole fish before roasting, or made into hummus (see page 26).

## Oils, butter, and margarine

What oil to use when? Choose a vegetable oil like canola when the oil is merely a cooking aid. Olive oil is the preferred oil for pasta dishes and baking — use extra virgin olive oil only when the oil is really important to the dish like in oil-based sauces (see page 32) or in salad dressings. Walnut oil also works well in salads as it is strongly flavored. Use peanut oil in Asian-inspired dishes. Sesame oil can make all the difference to a dish but use very sparingly as it is surprisingly strong.

Don't be fooled into thinking light oil is lower in calories/kilojoules or more "healthy"; the word "light" refers only to the flavor which does not have the fullness of other oils and so the oil can be used unobtrusively.

Oil is recommended for most cooking, but if you want the taste of butter when frying (with eggs or onions, for example), try melting a spoonful of butter with vegetable oil which will stop it from burning. Butter should be kept in the refrigerator to ensure long-life and can be frozen for 6 months or more.

A hint — if you have run out of oil, butter, and margarine, most foods (such as onion, vegetables, garlic, herbs, and spices) can be "steamed" in a few tablespoons of water in a pan.

## Cheese

Parmesan or Romano cheese is a must-have. The pre-grated cheese available in containers bears little resemblance to the fresh version, and is not a decent substitute in recipes. Best to buy a big block of fresh cheese, keep a little whole in the refrigerator then coarsely grate the remainder and store in tightly sealed containers in the refrigerator or freezer (it won't actually "freeze", by the way).

Other cheeses can be wrapped in foil or waxed greaseproof paper, sealed in a plastic bag, and stored in the vegetable compartment of the refrigerator or in a plastic container. If mold starts to form, slice off the cheese from about ½ inch (1 cm) under the area; the remaining cheese should be unaffected.

Feta can be purchased in long-life sealed packets which are handy to have on hand, as is a camembert or brie in a sealed can. Ricotta and cottage cheese, pre-packaged in small tubs, also have a fairly long life, and cream cheese even longer. Of course, these packaged cheeses aren't of the same quality as those consumed fresh but they are extremely practical. Processed slices of cheese seem to last forever but they aren't really suitable for more than toasted sandwiches.

Goats cheese from France, also known as chevre, is a boon to the after-work cook. Sealed packages of the white, crumbly cheese last for weeks, and it has a wonderful flavor and texture that can lift everyday food above the ordinary (see page 40).

*Eggs*

Refrigerated eggs in their cardboard box will keep for weeks, if not months. Store away from strong-smelling foods as the eggs will absorb the smell.

**TO MAKE PERFECT SCRAMBLED EGGS**

Lightly beat together eggs, cream or milk (use 1 tablespoon for every 2 eggs), and a pinch of salt. Melt 1 tablespoon butter in a heavy-based frying pan until it just begins to foam. Pour in eggs and cook very, very slowly over a low heat, stirring gently. The eggs will become creamy and soft. Serve on toasted bread or pumpernickel with strips of smoked salmon on top, a sprinkling of chopped chives, a spoonful of fish roe, and a good grinding of black pepper.

*What to cook when friends drop in*

Feeding unexpected guests isn't a problem if you have a well-stocked pantry. Conjure up a selection of antipasto from the cupboard, and serve with toasted bread (from the freezer) and crackers:

- sundried tomatoes, peppers (capsicum), and eggplant (aubergine)
- marinated artichokes
- bottled olives
- packaged halloumi cheese (drizzled with olive oil and lemon juice, sprinkled with dried oregano and freshly ground pepper and then broiled or grilled)
- packaged goats cheese (chevre)
- packaged feta
- cured meats (salami, smoked salmon, or trout)
- pesto
- tapenade
- canned beans (cannellini, pinto)

For a more substantial meal, try a risotto (see page 28) or a pasta with a pantry-assortment sauce (see page 36) olive oil and garlic (see page 32), or lemon (see page 34). The BLT pasta (see page 44) is great for planned entertaining.

*What to cook when you think you have nothing*

When you haven't been near a store in weeks, it is still possible to construct a dinner from a few items lurking at the back of the cupboard. Take a look at the following recipes for some ideas:

- Spiced Couscous with Fruit and Nuts, page 30
- Pasta with Olive Oil and Garlic, page 32
- Spiced Lentils, page 64
- Tuna and Beans, page 66
- Simple Onion Soup, page 76

*What to cook when you really can't be bothered*

There will always be a place for home-delivered food and frozen TV dinners, and sometimes a piece of toast, instant noodles, or some perfect scrambled eggs (see page 11) is all you really want. There are, however, a few alternatives that only involve minimum effort. For example:

- Soy Chili Sauce on a Stir-Fry, page 18
- Pesto on Pasta, page 22
- Spiced Couscous with Fruit and Nuts, page 30
- Thai Beef Salad, page 88
- Pizza, page 98
- Salmon with Green Vegetables, page 96
- Baked Parcels, page 102

*What to cook when you're really hungry*

Some of the recipes in this book take a little longer to cook but they don't require much effort to prepare and they will provide a meal to satisfy a ravenous hunger on those nights when you haven't come home with an armful of fresh ingredients. Try one of these:

- Spaghetti Carbonara, page 38
- Macaroni Cheese, page 46
- Baked Potatoes with Fillings, page 54
- Easy-to-Make Laksa, page 78
- Peasant Bean Soup, page 80

*What to have for dessert*

There are no dessert recipes included in the book. If you keep icecream in the freezer and chocolate somewhere to hand, why bother with any more effort?

# What to stock in your kitchen

## ON THE SHELF

### In cans

artichoke hearts

bean sprouts

beans — cannellini, red kidney, borlotti, haricot (navy)

chick peas (garbanzo beans)

coconut milk — canned, powdered or in a block

corn — kernels, baby corn

crabmeat

fish — tuna, salmon, sardines, anchovies

fruit — apricots, peaches, cherries, pears

lentils

mushrooms - champignons, straw mushrooms

tomatoes — whole peeled, passata

### In bottles and packets

stock — chicken, beef, vegetable, fish

clams

olives

capers

tapenade (olive paste)

tahini

pesto

sundried vegetables — peppers (capsicum), tomatoes, eggplant (aubergine)

pickled vegetables — antipasto, dill cucumbers, onions

minced chili (sambal olek)

minced ginger

minced garlic

blanchan (shrimp paste)

curry paste — Indian, Thai red and green

sauces — tomato ketchup, sweet chili, hot chili pepper, soy (light and dark), teriyaki, nam pla (fish sauce), worcestershire, hoi sin, oyster, plum

pickles and chutneys

mirin (rice wine) or dry sherry

vinegars — cider, red wine, rice wine, balsamic

oils — olive, extra virgin olive, peanut, walnut, sesame, all-purpose vegetable

whole-egg mayonnaise

mustards — dijon, whole-grain

honey

peanut butter

berry jam

## Dry goods

noodles — rice vermicelli, Chinese egg, fresh soy noodles

pasta — penne, linguine, fettucine, spaghetti, lasagne, macaroni

rice — long-grain white, arborio, brown, wild

couscous

cornmeal (polenta)

dried breadcrumbs

corn tortilla chips, taco shells

crackers

dried fruit — golden raisins (sultanas), raisins, dates, figs, apricots, prunes

nuts — pine nuts, peanuts, walnuts, cashews, almonds, hazelnuts, pistachio

seeds — poppy, sesame

dried mushrooms — shiitake, porcini

herbs and spices — thyme, oregano, basil, sage, coriander, tumeric, dill rosemary, cayenne pepper, paprika, saffron, allspice, garam masala, cinnamon, cloves, cardamom, cumin, salt — cooking and sea salt flakes

pepper — black peppercorns, white

sugar — white, caster, brown or palm

flour — all-purpose (plain) and self-rising white flour

cornstarch (cornflour)

baking powder (bicarbonate of soda)

shredded coconut

dry yeast

## IN THE REFRIGERATOR

cheese — blue, cheddar, mozzarella, ricotta, feta, parmesan, camembert, goats (chevre)

chocolate

milk

cream, sour cream

cured meat — salami, bacon, pancetta, smoked salmon

eggs

lemons, limes

packaged tortillas or pita bread

wholewheat (wholemeal) flour

yogurt

## IN THE FREEZER

berries

bread

broad beans

butter

icecream

pastry — shortcrust, filo, puff

peas

pizza base

spinach

## IN A DARK PANTRY

garlic

ginger

onions — white, brown, Spanish (purple)

potatoes

pumpkin

sweet potato (kumera)

## A SELECTION OF FRESH INGREDIENTS

broccoli

cucumber

eggplants (aubergines)

English spinach

green beans

mushrooms

peppers (capsicums)

scallions (spring onions/shallots)

snow peas (mange tout)

tomatoes

zucchini (courgettes)

salad greens *

lean meat, chicken, fish

---

* invest in a lettuce crisper — a washed and dried iceberg lettuce with the heart removed can last for up to 1 month. Remove the heart by banging the end hard on a benchtop, then twisting out.

# Potato wedges with aioli

*As a side dish or comforting indulgence, those few dirty potatoes hanging at the bottom of the cupboard can be transformed into something truly uplifting. Aim to make them crispy on the outside, and soft on the inside. For the aioli, you must use whole-egg mayonnaise; it is widely available. The garlic taste is strong and robust; try it at this strength and increase the mayonnaise if you want it milder. Aioli can be kept in a cool, dark place for several weeks.*

*Preparation 5 minutes*
*Cooking time 40 minutes*

## INGREDIENTS

waxy, white-fleshed potatoes — 6 large, scrubbed clean
salt — 1 tspn
all-purpose (plain) flour — 4 tbpsns
paprika — 1 tspn
cayenne pepper — ½ tspn

olive oil or melted butter — 2 tbspns
salt and freshly ground black pepper — to serve
aioli — to serve
salsa — to serve (optional)

## TO MAKE

1. Place potatoes in boiling salted water and cook until just tender but not too soft, about 15-20 minutes.
2. Drain, peel and slice each potato into quarters lengthwise to form wedges. Pat dry with a cloth.
3. Preheat oven to 400°F (200°C/Gas 4).
4. Mix salt, flour, paprika, and cayenne pepper in a large bowl. Toss wedges first in oil or butter to coat, then in flour mixture.
6. Bake in a baking dish about 20 minutes, turning after 10 minutes, until crispy and golden brown.
7. Serve sprinkled with salt and pepper, and accompanied by aioli and salsa.

*Aioli*

For aoili, start with 2 cloves crushed garlic whipped into about ¾ cup (6 fl oz/180 ml) whole-egg mayonnaise. Add a pinch of salt and a generous squeeze of lemon juice to taste.

Try adding sweet chili sauce or zest of lime for something different. Serve at room temperature.

# Peanut saté sauce

This thick nutty sauce can be made in advance and stored in the refrigerator to be served in a variety of ways. Don't be intimidated by the shrimp paste; it's a useful pantry ingredient and is that missing something between the sauces you love in restaurants and the ones you may have tried to make at home. A hint: if the peanut butter is too thick and hard to work with, pop the opened jar into the microwave 20 seconds or into hot water for a minute or two to soften.

Preparation 2 minutes
Cooking time 15 minutes

## INGREDIENTS

*Makes 1 cup*

peanut oil — 2 tbspns
onion — 1, finely chopped
garlic — 1 large clove, crushed
ginger — crushed, 1 tspn
peanut butter — 6 tbspns
coconut milk or chicken stock — ⅓ cup
   (3 fl oz/90 ml)

blachan (shrimp paste) — ½ tspn (optional)
soy sauce — 1 tbspn or to taste
palm sugar or brown sugar — 2 tspns
minced chili (sambal olek) — ¼ tspn or
   to taste
lemon juice — 1 tspn

## TO MAKE

1. Place oil, onion, garlic, and ginger in small saucepan over medium heat and fry until onion is soft.
2. Blend in peanut butter and coconut milk.
3. Mix in remaining ingredients and simmer over low heat 5-10 minutes to develop.
4. Serve warm or at room temperature.

## VARIATIONS

• *Use coconut milk rather than stock if you want a richer, creamier sauce.*
• *For a runnier sauce, dilute with hot water.*
• *If you can't use shrimp paste, try adding fish sauce (nam pla) to taste.*
• *For extra nuttiness, add a couple of tablespoons crushed peanuts with onions.*

## SERVING SUGGESTIONS

• *Peanut sauce works well on chicken, beef, or pork satés. Cut meat into 1 in. (2 cm) cubes, thread onto bamboo skewers that have been soaked in water, and broil, grill, or barbecue until cooked through. You can prepare them in advance and marinate the meat for several hours or overnight in a mixture of peanut or olive oil, chopped garlic, and ginger.*
• *You can also serve the sauce warm over steamed vegetables and rice. Or try your own variation of the Indonesian dish gado gado, which uses slices of cold vegetables covered with warm sauce: try a mixture of lettuce or cabbage, cucumber, carrot, tomato, boiled potato, hard-cooked (boiled) eggs, blanched snow-peas (mange tout) and broccoli.*

# Soy chili sauce

*The ingredients for this sauce form the basis for many Asian sauces. Adjust the amounts to suit your taste. You can also experiment with the addition of oyster sauce, mushroom soy sauce, and shrimp paste (blachan). The sesame oil provides a great nutty taste but it is strong so use sparingly.*

*Preparation 2 minutes*

## INGREDIENTS

*Makes 1/2 cup*

garlic — 1 small clove
salt — pinch
sugar — ½ tspn, optional
soy sauce — 3 tbpsns
sesame or peanut oil — 2 tspns

water — 2 tbspns
mirin (rice wine) or dry sherry — 2 tbspns
minced chili or chili sauce — ½ tspn
ginger — grated, ½ tspn

## TO MAKE

1. Crush garlic with salt and sugar in a small bowl.
2. Mix in remaining ingredients.
3. Use sauce cold or warmed in a saucepan or microwave.

## VARIATIONS

• *If using a sweet chili sauce, you may wish to leave out the sugar.*
• *A sweeter, sticker marinade for meat or chicken can be made with honey. Omit the sugar and add 2 teaspoons honey (or to taste) with the soy sauce. Marinate meat overnight if possible, before broiling, grilling, or barbecueing*
• *Add 1 tablespoon each chopped scallions (spring onions/shallots) and toasted sesame seeds.*

## SERVING SUGGESTIONS

• *Broiled or grilled kebabs, chicken pieces, and fish can be dipped into this sauce.*
• *Use as a sauce when stir-frying meat or vegetables. Remember when stir-frying meat to slice meat thinly and across the grain and to cook it in batches (overcrowding the pan will cause the meat to stew and toughen).*
• *Splash the sauce onto a bowl of noodles or fried rice.*

# Tomato sauce

*If you can master this simple sauce, you have the makings of hundreds of afterwork meals. There are so many uses for this sauce, it is practical to make a full quantity and store it in airtight containers in the refrigerator for about 1 week, or freeze it in usable portions. Be careful not to burn the garlic which would make your sauce bitter.*

**Preparation 5 minutes**
**Cooking time 35 minutes**

## INGREDIENTS

*Makes about 3 cups*

peeled tomatoes — 2 x 14 oz (440 g) cans
extra virgin olive oil — 2 tbspns
garlic — 1 clove, finely chopped
onion — 1, finely chopped
tomato paste — 1 tbpsn
sugar — ½ tspn

salt and freshly ground black pepper
bay leaf — 1
basil — 1 tbspn chopped fresh, or
    1 tspn dried
parsley — chopped, 1 tbspn

## TO MAKE

1. Puree tomatoes in a food processor. Remove seeds by pouring puree through a sieve into a bowl.
2. Heat oil and garlic in saucepan over medium heat until garlic is fragrant, about 1 minute.
3. Add onion and cook gently until soft.
3. Add pureed tomatoes, tomato paste, sugar, salt and pepper, and bay leaf. Simmer gently about 20 minutes.
4. Remove bay leaf and add basil and parsley. Cook 5-10 more minutes until slightly thickened.
5. Serve immediately, or allow to cool to room temperature and store.

## SERVING SUGGESTIONS

• *Serve hot over pasta.*
• *Serve hot as a sauce over panfried, grilled, broiled, or barbecued meat or fish.*
• *Serve at room temperature as a dip for crudité.*
• *Add stock and vegetables to form a soup.*

## VARIATIONS

• *If you want to make the best possible sauce, use 2 lb (1 kg) very ripe tomatoes —the redder and softer, the better. Prepare tomatoes by placing them in a bowl upside down and using a knife to slash a cross mark on the flesh at their ends. Cover with boiling water. After a few minutes the skin should start to lift back from the flesh at the slash marks. Remove tomatoes from water with slotted spoon and peel the skins off — best done on a chopping board or over a bowl. You can now remove the seeds. Puree the pulp or chop roughly.*
• *You can skip removing the seeds or pureeing the tomatoes to save time but the taste and texture won't be as good.*
• *Use a few sprigs of fresh oregano or 1 teaspoon dried, instead of basil.*
• *For a spicier sauce, add cayenne pepper or hot paprika to taste. Alternatively, add a couple of chopped, seeded chilis with the garlic — you may also wish to increase the garlic to 2 cloves.*

# Pesto

Preparation 5 minutes

Pesto is primarily used as a pasta sauce in Italy — a serious limitation to its potential. It's a must-have in your kitchen — buy it if you don't feel like making it yourself. Made from fresh basil (never dried), it's really simple to throw together and will keep in the refrigerator for weeks if stored in a sealed jar with a layer of olive oil on top. The taste is fairly rich, so you don't need to use much. Serve the sauce at room temperature, rather than chilled.

## INGREDIENTS

garlic — 2 large cloves, crushed
salt — pinch
pine nuts — 2 tbspns
fresh basil leaves — 2 cups
parmesan — 2 oz (60 g), grated
extra virgin olive oil — 5 tbspns

## TO MAKE

1. Mash garlic with salt in a small bowl.
2. Process pine nuts, basil, and parmesan in a food processor with 1 tablespoon olive oil. Add garlic.
3. With the motor running, pour in remaining oil in a steady stream, so that the pesto becomes a plump smooth paste.

## VARIATIONS

• Try toasting the pine nuts first. Spread them out on a baking tray and place in a medium oven or under the broiler (grill). Shake the tray every minute or two to ensure even cooking — be careful that they don't burn.
• Instead of parmesan, use another hard Italian cheese such as pecorino.

## SERVING SUGGESTIONS

• Pesto obviously belongs on pasta — on its own or tossed with extra toasted pine nuts, sundried tomato, roasted peppers (capsicums) or eggplant (aubergine), or crumbled ricotta.
• Spread it warm as a base for sandwiches, pizzas, and focaccias, so that the olive oil and cheese melt and soak in.
• Add a scoop of pesto to your boiled potatoes or beans, instead of butter.
• Use it instead of mint jelly with roast lamb or broiled (grilled) lamb chops.
• Toss it into a pan with stir-fried beef, along with a handful of black olives, a few sundried vegetables (tomatoes, peppers, eggplant/ aubergine), and a splash of wine. Serve on hot polenta or short pasta.
• Add a dollop to soups such as minestrone or peasant bean soup (see page 80).

# Creamy cheese salsa

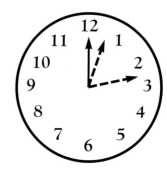

Hot or cold, this salsa is thick and not quite smooth which makes it great comfort food. Cheddar, gruyere, or emmenthal all work well in this recipe but are best melted in a double boiler. You can improvize one by half-filling a large saucepan with water, and placing a smaller one inside it. Heat water to a simmer then add ingredients to small pan.

Preparation 2 minutes
Cooking time 10 minutes

## INGREDIENTS

*Makes 3 cups*

butter — $\frac{1}{2}$ tbspn
ricotta or cottage cheese — $1\frac{1}{2}$ cups
grated cheese — 1 cups
sour cream — $\frac{1}{2}$ cup
salt and pepper

## TO MAKE

1. Melt butter in double boiler.
2. Add all other ingredients and stir continuously until cheese melts and sauce is thick, about 5-10 minutes.
3. Serve immediately or let cool, depending on how you plan to use it.

## VARIATIONS

• *Mexican variation* — add $\frac{1}{4}$ teaspoon cumin, $\frac{1}{4}$ teaspoon ground oregano, and hot pepper sauce (tabasco, for example) to taste.
• *Blue cheese variation* — add 1 oz (30 g) grated parmesan and 2 oz (60 g) blue cheese instead of, or in addition to, grated cheese.
• *Mustard variation* — add $\frac{1}{2}$ teaspoon dijon mustard.

## SERVING SUGGESTIONS

• *Spoon hot sauce over steamed vegetables and baked potatoes*
• *Let cool and thicken and use as a dip for crudités or corn tortilla chips.*

# Hummus

Preparation 5 minutes

This Lebanese dip has a smooth nutty taste due to the tahini (see page 10) which makes it a great neutral "accessory" for meat and vegetables. Adjust the lemon juice to taste; like the garlic, it should not be overpowering. Hummus is usually served at room temperature or incorporated into other recipes. It can also be bought already made.

## INGREDIENTS

Makes 1½ cups

garlic — 2 cloves, crushed
salt — 1 tspn
tahini (sesame paste) — 1½ tbspns
lemon — 1- 2, juiced
chick peas — 5 oz (150 g) can, drained

## TO MAKE

1. Mash garlic with salt in a small bowl.
2. Blend tahini, juice, and garlic in a food processor.
3. Add chick peas and puree until smooth.

## SERVING SUGGESTIONS

• Hummus keeps well and makes an interesting base for bread and pizzas. It teams beautifully with either tomato, roasted pepper (capsicum) or eggplant (aubergine), or a combination of these. It also lifts a salad sandwich.
• Serve as a dip with a good bread, such as Turkish pidé, or with hot or cold meatballs, preferably made from lamb. Traditionally, the dip is served spooned onto a flat plate, and spread out to cover most of the base. Drizzle over some extra virgin olive oil and sprinkle with cayenne pepper.

• Try a spoonful of hummus with fish, such as panfried trout, or spread it on a whole fish before baking.
• Add a Middle Eastern twist on an old classic — sausages and mashed potatoes. Add a generous spoonful of hummus to the potatoes when mashing (see page 5), and serve with broiled or grilled spicy sausages and a salad of bitter greens.

# Simplified risotto

*Rather than relying on endless stirring, a good risotto can be made with these shortcuts. Experiment with ingredients, but the main rules are to use only arborio rice, coat it well in oil first, ensure the stock is boiling when adding, and eat immediately, as the dish starts to become gluggy very quickly. Ingredients that need cooking should be cooked first, flavoring should be added with the rice, and any ingredient that can't take 20 minutes of steaming should be added later so as not to overcook.*

Preparation 5 minutes
Cooking time 20 minutes

## INGREDIENTS

*Serves 4*
olive oil — ¼ cup
bacon — 2 strips (rashers), chopped
sage — 6 leaves, chopped
chicken or vegetable stock — 3 cups

arborio rice — 2 cups
cannellini beans — 14 oz (440 g) can
black pepper — freshly ground
parmesan — to serve (optional)

## TO MAKE

1. Add olive oil, most of the bacon, and half the sage to a saucepan and fry over medium heat until bacon is almost cooked.
2. Meanwhile, bring stock to boil in another saucepan.
3. Add rice to saucepan with bacon and stir for a few minutes until well coated in oil.
4. Pour boiling stock into pan with rice, return to boil, and cover. Reduce heat to low and simmer 20 minutes.
5. Meanwhile, add remaining oil, bacon, and sage to a pan and fry for a couple of minutes. Add beans and simmer over very low heat until rice is ready.
6. Uncover rice and stir. If stock has not been fully absorbed, cover and cook for a few more minutes. Spoon onto plates then pile bean mixture on top. Grind black pepper over and add shavings of parmesan if desired. Serve immediately.

## VARIATIONS

• *Add a tablespoon of butter with the olive oil to risotto when you want a more buttery taste.*
• *The classic northern Italian dish known as risotto alla millanese is a pantry-only gem. Add ¼ cup white wine to the stock, bring to boil, and add a pinch of saffron threads or ½ teaspoon powdered saffron. When rice is cooked, stir in ½ cup freshly grated parmesan and 1 tablespoon butter before serving.*
• *Add a tablespoon of pesto to uncooked rice, and stir a few more spoonfuls through cooked risotto with a drizzle of olive oil.*
• *Soak ½ cup dried porcini mushrooms (see page 9) and add with the rice.*
• *Fry 8 oz (250 g) chicken fillet (cut into small pieces) with the onion at the start, and add a handful of chopped sun-dried tomatoes with the uncooked rice.*
• *Saute onion then add 2 chopped tomatoes and a few shredded basil leaves with the rice.*

# Spiced couscous with fruit and nuts

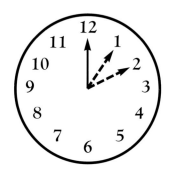

The perfect afterwork ingredient, precooked packaged couscous lasts indefinitely on the shelf and needs only soaking for a few minutes, rather than cooking, before eating. The time and water quantity may vary from brand to brand. This basic recipe provides a light meal using only pantry staples but you can add any fresh ingredients you have on hand. Use butter rather than oil or margarine for the flavor.

Preparation 5 minutes
Cooking time 5 minutes

## INGREDIENTS

*Serves 4*

pine nuts — ½ cup
couscous — 2 cups
boiling water — 1½ cups
salt — large pinch
butter — 1 tbspn

onion — 1, finely chopped
ground cinnamon — ½ tspn
currants or raisins — ¼ cup
dried apricots — ½ cup, chopped
extra butter — 3 tbspns in pieces

## TO MAKE

1. Toast pine nuts in a dry heavy-based frying pan. Set aside.
2. Place couscous in a large bowl, pour in boiling water and stir in salt. Let stand about 3-5 minutes until water is absorbed.
3. Meanwhile, melt 1 tablespoon butter in frying pan. Add onion and fry until soft.
4. Stir in spices, dried fruit, and pine nuts.
5. Mix pieces of butter through warm couscous with a fork to fluff it up.
Add onion spice mixture, stir through and serve.

## VARIATIONS

• *To make this a heartier meal, you could add 8 oz (250 g) lean ground (minced) beef or sliced lamb or chicken. Fry the meat with the onion.*
• *Instead of meat — or along with it — add slices of zucchini (courgette) and carrot, strips of red pepper (capsicum), cubes of eggplant (aubergine), or a cup of canned chick peas (garbanzo beans).*
• *Try a teaspoon of cumin and/or ground coriander instead of the cinnamon.*
• *Add chopped walnuts or sliced almonds instead of pine nuts.*
• *If you have time, soak the dried fruit in water to cover for an hour so they plump up.*

# Pasta with olive oil and garlic

*Don't think that you have to pile a whole load of ingredients or sauces onto pasta to make it a meal because the greatest thing about pasta is that it tastes its best when cooked carefully and treated simply. Try this recipe if you really think that your kitchen is bare, and you'll realise you can feast on almost nothing.*

Preparation 3 minutes
Cooking time 12 minutes

## INGREDIENTS

*Serves 4*
extra virgin olive oil — 6 tbspns
garlic — 5 cloves, slivered
pasta — 1 lb (500 g)

black pepper — freshly ground
parmesan — shavings (optional)
parsley — chopped (optional)

## TO MAKE

1. Place olive oil and garlic in small pan over very low heat. Heat slowly until the garlic is just turning golden brown — the oil will be infused with garlic, so you can discard all or some of the slivers if desired.
2. Meanwhile, cook pasta until al dente, usually 5-12 minutes (see page 4 for advice).
3. The moment pasta is cooked, drain and place in large serving bowl. Pour garlicky olive oil over the top and toss well.
4. Serve with lots of freshly ground black pepper and shavings of parmesan or chopped parsley if desired.

## VARIATIONS

• *You can add a sliced chili with the garlic.*
• *Or halve the quantity of garlic and add 100 g (4 oz) chopped anchovy fillets instead.*

# Pasta with lemon

*Once again, this simple dish involves minimal ingredients but will taste best if they are of good quality — good olive oil, freshly squeezed lemon juice, and freshly grated parmesan.*

**Preparation 3 minutes**
**Cooking time up to 15 minutes**

## INGREDIENTS

*Serves 4*
extra virgin olive oil — ½ cup
garlic — 2 cloves, crushed
fresh parsley — chopped, 1 cup
lemon juice — 4 tbspns

pasta — 1 lb (500 g)
parmesan — freshly grated, 4 tbspns
black pepper — freshly ground

## TO MAKE

1. Place oil, garlic, and parsley in small saucepan over low heat, and cook until garlic is fragrant, about 1 minute.
2. Remove from heat, add lemon juice and set aside.
3. Cook pasta until al dente, usually 5-12 minutes (see page 4). Drain, and return to warm saucepan with a dash of olive oil.
4. Heat lemon sauce (if necessary) and pour over pasta. Toss with parmesan and black pepper.

## VARIATION

• *A bit of lemon zest can add extra tang.*
• *Along with the lemon juice, add 7 oz (200 g) can solid-packed tuna, drained and broken up with a fork. Parmesan is optional.*
• *If adding tuna, you may also like to add a dash of worcestershire or hot pepper sauce and even a handful of chopped walnuts.*
• *Along with the lemon juice, add 7 oz (200 g) can crabmeat, instead of tuna, drained and broken up with a fork. Do not add parmesan to this sauce.*

# The pantry assortment pasta sauce

*Put together these cupboard ingredients in whatever combinations take your fancy, depending on taste and availability. Throw in the whole lot if you want!*

*Preparation 3 minutes*
*Cooking time 12 minutes*

## INGREDIENTS

pasta — 1 lb (500 g)
olive oil — 2 tbspns
A combination of:
    garlic — 1-2 cloves, finely chopped
    onion — 1, finely chopped
    chilies — fresh or minced, to taste

peeled tomatoes — 1 or 2 x
    14 oz (400 g) cans
anchovy fillets — 2-6, chopped
capers — 1-3 tbspns, chopped
black olives — ½-1 cup, pitted (stoned)
tuna — 7 oz (200 g) can, drained

## TO MAKE

1. Put pasta on to cook, usually
5-12 minutes (see page 4 for advice).
2. Meanwhile, add the ingredients that need "cooking" to olive oil in small pan — such as garlic or onion, if using.
3. Add chilies and tomatoes, if using, and simmer over low heat for a few minutes until tomatoes soften and reduce.

4. Add any other ingredients and heat through. Let stand if you have time to allow the flavors to mingle.
5. Toss sauce through cooked, drained pasta.

# Spaghetti carbonara

The heat of the pasta "cooks" the eggs in this dish; serve it immediately or it will start to get gluggy. Use whatever pasta you have on hand but this sauce works best with long thin ribbons which it can stick to, such as linguine and fettuccine. A good quality oil provides important flavor, and using pancetta will make all the difference.

Preparation 5 minutes
Cooking time 15 minutes

## INGREDIENTS

*Serves 4*
spaghetti — 500 g (1 lb)
extra virgin olive oil — 4 tbspns
garlic — 2 large cloves, finely chopped
red chilies — 4, seeded and sliced (optional)

bacon or pancetta — 125 g (4 oz), chopped
eggs — 2, lightly beaten
parmesan — freshly grated, ½ cup
black pepper — freshly ground

## TO MAKE

1. Cook pasta until al dente, usually 5-12 minutes (see page 4 for advice).
2. Meanwhile, add oil, garlic, chili, and bacon to a large frying pan and cook over low heat for a few minutes until garlic is pale golden and bacon has cooked.
3. Drain pasta; add immediately to frying pan. Take pan off heat and immediately add eggs and parmesan. Toss through, allowing the heat of the pasta to "cook" the eggs and parmesan.
4. Grind loads of pepper over the pasta and serve immediately.

## VARIATIONS

• *For a thinner but richer sauce, use egg yolks only. Beat 4 yolks with a couple of tablespoons of single (light, runny) cream.*
• *Use thin strips of ham or prosciutto instead of bacon.*
• *Add chopped onion with the garlic.*
• *Add sliced mushrooms instead of, or along with, the bacon. You could add 1 cup peas too.*
• *Blanched fresh asparagus or a drained can of asparagus is a good addition. Add to the frying pan after the bacon has cooked and toss to warm through.*
• *Pecorino romano is a good substitute for parmesan. In a pinch, you can use other cheeses but it will be a compromise on taste, and the texture will be thicker — more like macaroni and cheese.*

# Pasta with roasted eggplant

*Goats cheese, or chevre as it is known in France, is a white, crumbly cheese that can be bought in sealed packages that last for months in the refrigerator. Penne or rigatoni is a good pasta to choose for this dish.*

Preparation 10 minutes
Cooking time 15 minutes

## INGREDIENTS

*Serves 4*

eggplant (aubergine) — 1 large
salt
olive oil — about 2 tbspns total
garlic — 1-2 cloves, chopped

pasta — 1 lb (500 g)
Italian tomato sauce or passata — 1 cup
goats cheese — 3½ oz (100 g)

## TO MAKE

1. Cut eggplant lengthwise into thin slices. Sprinkle liberally with salt and let stand for a few minutes to disgorge juices. Pat with paper towels.
2. Place eggplant slices on tray under broiler (grill), brush with about 1 tablespoon olive oil and sprinkle with garlic. Cook under high heat until very brown, about 15 minutes, turning to cook both sides and brushing occasionally with more olive oil.
3. Meanwhile, boil pasta until al dente. Drain; return to hot saucepan with tomato sauce and toss.
4. Cut eggplant into strips and toss through pasta with crumbled goats cheese.

## VARIATIONS

• *You can use store-bought tomato sauce or make your own (see page 20).*
• *Add a spoonful of home-made or store-bought pesto (see page 22) or tapenade if desired.*
• *Try shavings of parmesan or cubes of feta instead of goats cheese. Or top each serving with a large spoonful of ricotta.*

# Pasta with roasted red peppers and artichokes

*It's the red, rather than green, peppers that you want for this recipe as the cooking process makes them deliciously sweet. Penne or rigatoni pasta is recommended.*

**Preparation 2 minutes**
**Cooking time 20 minutes**

## INGREDIENTS

*Serves 4*

red peppers (capsicums)— 3 large, halved lengthwise and seeded
pasta — 1 lb (500 g)
olive oil — 4 tbspns
garlic — 1 clove, finely chopped

marinated artichoke hearts — 12 oz (375 g) jar, undrained
sardines — 4 oz (125 g) can, torn into pieces
black pepper — cracked
parmesan — shavings (optional)

## TO MAKE

1. Place peppers on tray under hot broiler (grill), skin side up, and cook under high heat until the skin blackens and bubbles. Let cool slightly, peel off skin and cut peppers into strips.
2. Place olive oil and garlic in a pan and cook over medium heat until garlic is fragrant, about 1 minute.
3. Halve artichoke hearts and add to pan with 6 tablespoons marinade and red pepper strips. Saute gently over very low heat while cooking pasta. Add sardines and heat through.
4. Cook pasta until al dente, usually 5-12 minutes (see page 4). Toss with artichoke, peppers, sardines and oil. Serve with cracked pepper and parmesan shavings.

## VARIATIONS

• *Add a handful of chopped black olives or a dollop of tapendade for extra impact visually and on the palate.*
• *Instead of parmesan, crumble goats cheese on top.*
• *You can make a pantry-only special by tossing strips of canned pimiento pepper with the artichoke instead of fresh red pepper.*

# BLT *pasta*

Inspired by the bacon, lettuce, and tomato sandwich combos, this may not be the quickest of recipes but it involves almost no effort and will hold its own against anything you can get in a restaurant — perfect for afterwork entertaining.

*Preparation 5 minutes*
*Cooking time 1 hour*

## INGREDIENTS

*Serves 4*
tomatoes — 8 large
basil or oregano — dried, 2 tspns
garlic — 2 cloves, chopped
bacon — 4 strips (rashers), chopped
olive oil — 4 tbspns
salt and freshly ground black pepper
English spinach — 1 bunch
pasta — 1 lb (500 g)

## TO MAKE

1. Preheat oven to 400°F (200°C/Gas 6).
2. Cut tomatoes in half and place (cut side up) in baking dish. Scatter with basil, garlic, and bacon. Drizzle with olive oil. Season with salt and pepper. Bake for 50-60 minutes until very soft.
3. When tomatoes are almost done, put pasta on to boil.
4. Rinse spinach and remove thick stalks. Place in heavy saucepan, cover tightly, and cook over low heat, stirring frequently until it begins to wilt, about 3 minutes. Cover and cook 1-2 more minutes until tender. Squeeze out extra moisture.
5. Drain cooked pasta and place in a large bowl. Break up tomatoes roughly and add, along with pan juices, to pasta. Add spinach and toss.

## VARIATION

• *Serve with shavings of parmesan if desired.*
• *Throw a handful of black olives into the baking dish as well.*
• *Alternatively, you can roast a whole head of garlic (see page 9) with the tomatoes for a really earthy dish.*
• *Instead of bacon, serve the tomatoes with slices of prosciutto that have been crisped under the broiler (grill).*
• *If you want to make it even simpler, forget the bacon and spinach altogether.*
• *Make up the tomatoes and garlic alone and serve with crusty bread, instead of pasta, to soak up the juices.*

# Macaroni cheese

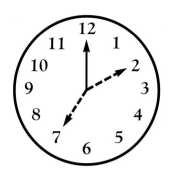

Here are a few handy, more "adult" suggestions for this ultimate comfort food. An ideal meal when life (particularly shopping and cooking) seems a bit too hard. The walnuts add a wonderful crunch to this ricotta version. It is a dish for those who prefer mild flavors — for more bite, add prepared or dry mustard to the white sauce to taste
The cheese should be one that melts well and also provides good flavor — mature cheddar, swiss, american, gruyere, or a combination. A short pasta like rigatoni or small pasta shells is recommended.

*Preparation 10 minutes*
*Cooking time 25 minutes*

## INGREDIENTS
*Serves 2-3*

pasta — 8 oz (250 g), cooked until al dente
butter — 2 tbspns
flour — 1-2 tbspns
milk — 1½ cups
salt and pepper

ricotta cheese — ⅓ cup
cheese — grated, ⅔ cup
chives — chopped, 4 tbspns
garlic — 1 clove
walnut pieces — 1 cup (about 4 oz/125 g)

## TO MAKE

1. Preheat oven to 450°F (220°C/Gas 6).
2. Melt butter in a saucepan, sprinkle in 1 tablespoon flour. Stir with a whisk to form a smooth paste, adding more flour if necessary. Keep stirring until it browns a little. Pour in milk gradually, stirring constantly. Add salt and pepper, and continue to stir until sauce thickens.

3. Mix in ricotta, half of the grated cheese, and chives. Fold cooked pasta into sauce.
4. Rub a buttered oven-proof casserole dish with cut garlic clove. Pour in pasta. Sprinkle with remaining cheese then walnuts.
5. Bake 15-20 minutes until walnuts have toasted and cheese has melted.

# Chili herb variation

## INGREDIENTS

*Serves 2-3*
butter — 2 tbspns
onion — 1, finely chopped
garlic — 1 clove, finely chopped
red chilies — 2-4, seeded and chopped
milk — 1 cup
egg — 1
salt — ½ tspn
black pepper — freshly ground

pasta — 8 oz (250 g), cooked until just
   al dente
cheese — grated, 2 cups
dried breadcrumbs — ½ cup
dried herbs (oregano or mixed) — 2 tspns
parmesan — grated, 2 tbspns
extra cheese — grated, ½ cup
butter — 2 tbspns, melted

## TO MAKE

1. Preheat oven to 350°F (180°C/Gas 3).
2. Melt butter in saucepan over medium heat. Fry onion, garlic, and chili until onion is soft.
3. Beat together milk, egg, salt, and pepper in a bowl.
4. Mix with cooked pasta, cheese, and onion mixture. Pour into greased oven-proof casserole dish.

5. Mix together breadcrumbs, herbs, parmesan, and extra cheese and scatter over pasta. Drizzle with melted butter.
6. Bake until top is golden brown, about 40 minutes.

*Beef stock variation*

## INGREDIENTS

*Serves 2-3*

butter — 1 tbspn
onion — 1 white, chopped
bacon — 1 slice (rasher), chopped (optional)
beef stock — 1½ cups
flour — 1 tbspn

flour — 1 tbspn
pasta — 8 oz (250 g), cooked until al dente
cheese — grated, ½ cup
parmesan — freshly grated, ½ cup
parsley — chopped, ½ cup

## TO MAKE

1. Preheat oven to 350°F (180°C/Gas 4).
2. Melt butter in large frying pan.
Add onion and bacon and cook until
onion is soft.
3. Pour in stock and sprinkle in flour. Bring
to boil then simmer until thickened slightly.

4. Mix in cooked pasta, grated cheese,
½ cup parmesan, and parsley. Pour into
a buttered oven-proof casserole dish.
Top with remaining parmesan.
5. Bake 15-20 minutes until cheese is
melted and golden brown.

# Indian noodle stir-fry

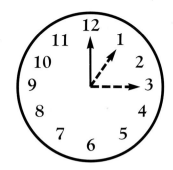

Preparation 5 minutes
Cooking time 10 minutes

*Yellow hokkein noodles can be bought fresh in sealed plastic bags from the refrigerated section of supermarkets, delis, and Chinese food stores. They'll keep refrigerated for over a week, even longer if frozen. Experiment with noodle dishes of your own, perhaps with a Soy Chili Sauce (see page 18). The process is the same:*
*(1) place noodles in boiling water for 30 seconds, then drain*
*(2) stir-fry vegetables, strips of meat or chicken, or a selection of seafood in a wok or large pan*
*(3) add sauces and spices, throw in the noodles, and toss the whole lot around for a few minutes to heat through.*
*Let stand for a few minutes to allow flavors to develop without overcooking. You may need a fair amount of oil and/or a dash of water to make noodles soft and slippery.*

## INGREDIENTS

*Serves 2-4*

peanut oil — 2 tbspns
onion — 1, chopped
tomato — 1, chopped
chives or scallions (spring onions/shallots) — chopped, 2 tbspns
curry paste — 2 tspns

tomato ketchup (sauce) — 1-2 tbspns
chili sauce or minced chili — 1 tbspn, or to taste
soy sauce — 2 tspns, preferrably light
hokkein egg noodles — 1 lb (500 g), cooked
stock or water — 2-4 tbspns
eggs — 2, lightly beaten (optional)

## TO MAKE

1. Heat oil in wok or large frying pan. Add onion and fry over medium heat until soft.
2. Add tomato and chives and cook for a few minutes.
3. Add curry paste, and sauces and simmer gently for a few minutes.
4. Add noodles and toss through to heat.
5. Pour beaten egg over and leave to set for about 45 seconds on hot noodles. Mix through and serve.

## VARIATIONS

• *As mentioned, add whatever takes your fancy. Raw vegetables or meat should be sautéed after, or with, the onion. Some suggestions to begin: blanched Chinese long (snake) beans cut into pieces, squares of tofu, 4 oz (125 g) raw peeled shrimp (prawns), cubes of boiled potato, green peas, bean sprouts, shredded lettuce or cabbage, sliced zucchini (courgette) and mushrooms, and strips of green pepper (capsicum).*

# Spicy peanut noodles

There are a few simple fresh ingredients in this recipe that make it a great light meal, prepared in minutes. You can also served it chilled as a salad. Use fresh or dry egg noodles or vermicelli rice noodles.

*Preparation 5 minutes*
*Cooking time 10 minutes*

## INGREDIENTS

*Serves 4*

Chinese noodles — 1 lb (500 g)
peanut oil — 1 tbspn
chicken fillet — 1 lb (500 g), cut into strips
crunchy peanut butter — 1 tbspn
lime — juice of ½ (optional)
sesame oil — 2 tbspns
fish sauce (nam pla) — ¼ cup

soy sauce — 2 tbspns
brown sugar — ½ tspn
garlic —2 cloves, minced
scallions (spring onions/shallots) —
    5, chopped
peanuts — chopped, ⅓ cup
cilantro (fresh coriander leaves) — to serve

## TO MAKE

1. Cook noodles in boiling water according to packet instructions. Drain.
2. Meanwhile, heat oil in a wok or large pan and sauté chicken strips.
3. Combine remaining ingredients in a small bowl. Add to chicken with cooked noodles and toss through.
4. Served warm, topped with chopped peanuts and cilantro.

## VARIATIONS

• *Sauté 8 oz (250 g) raw shrimp (prawns) instead of the chicken. Or use cooked shrimp and toss with drained noodles.*
• *Add 7 oz (200 g) fresh or canned bean sprouts for extra crunch.*
• *Add 1 tablespoon shrimp paste (blachan) instead of fish sauce, and chili flakes as desired for a really authentic taste.*

# Baked potatoes with fillings

*Baking takes a while so it is not ideal for a fast-feed, but it is simple and there's not much washing up. The potatoes can be prepared in advance and just warmed through when ready. Microwaving doesn't taste as good but it saves on time: prick each potato all over with a fork, place on paper towel and microwave on high until tender (about 5 minutes for 1 potato, 10 minutes for 4 — depending on size and oven power). Reheat filled potato for about 3 minutes.*

Preparation 2 minutes
Cooking time 65 minutes

## INGREDIENTS

very large oval waxy potatoes (see page 5),
    scrubbed but not peeled
choice of filling, about 2-3 tbspns each

## TO MAKE

1. Preheat oven to 400°F (200°C/Gas 4).
2. Place potatoes directly on the oven rack and bake 1 hour. Insert a skewer into the middle. If it slides in easily and comes out coated in potato, they are ready. Remove and let cool enough to handle.
3. While potatoes are cooking, prepare filling.
4. Cut potatoes in half lengthwise and scoop out the center, leaving about ¼ inch (0.5 cm) to form a shell inside. Mix potato flesh in a bowl with choice of filling.
5. Scoop potato back into skin casing and top with any garnish. Place on baking sheet and return to oven 5-10 minutes to warm through.

## FILLING SUGGESTIONS

• *Try some of the following combinations:*
— *drained canned tuna with aioli (page 14)*
— *drained canned tuna mixed with a dash of sesame oil, dash of vinegar, a spoonful of grated ginger and some sesame seeds*
— *pesto with parmesan and ricotta*
— *chopped fresh dill, diced hard-cooked (boiled) eggs, cottage cheese*
— *chopped salami, fried with diced tomato and green pepper (capsicum)*
— *sautéed onion, prepared mustard, and worcestershire sauce*
— *sautéed sliced leek and bacon pieces*
— *sautéed onion and tomato with basil*
— *diced ham, cubes of cheddar or mozzarella, and dried or fresh oregano*
— *crushed garlic, grated gruyere, dash of milk or cream, and cracked pepper*
— *chili beans (page 7), topped with sour cream, grated cheese, and guacamole to serve*

# Potato and pea curry

A faster-cooking version of a standard Indian potato and pea curry, the tried-and-true pantry savior — the cooking time will depend on the size of the pieces. Serve it with an Indian chutney or pickle. Of course, like all curries, it tastes even better the next day.

*Preparation 5 minutes*
*Cooking time 25 minutes*

## INGREDIENTS

*Serves 4*

potatoes — 1½ lb (750 g), peeled and
    cut into large chunks
vegetable oil — 2 tbspns
garlic — 2 cloves, finely chopped
onion — 1 medium, finely chopped
ginger — grated, 2 tspns
hot chili (such as sambel olek) — minced,
    2 tspns
cardamom seeds — cracked, ¼ tspn
cumin — ½ tspn
turmeric — 1 tspn

garam masala — ½ tspn
salt — 1 tspn
pepper — to taste
ground cinnamon — ¼ tspn
cloves — 3
bay leaf — 1
lemon juice — 1 tbspn
rice — 2 cups, to serve
frozen peas — 1 cup
water — 4 tbspns

## TO MAKE

1. Parboil potatoes in salted water for 10 minutes. Drain and set aside.
2. Heat oil in a large saucepan. Add garlic and onion and sauté until onion is soft.
3. Add spices and lemon juice and fry gently for a few minutes.
4. Put rice on to cook (see page 4 for advice).
5. Add potatoes, peas, and water to onion mixture and mix well to combine. Cover tightly and cook 10 minutes.
6. Serve hot with steamed rice.

## VARIATIONS

• *Add 1 teaspoon mustard seeds after cooking onion and fry until they start to pop.*
• *Use less potato and instead add 5 oz/150 g pumpkin, peeled and cut into large chunks. Add to boiling potatoes after 5 minutes.*
• *Before serving, sprinkle the curry with 4 tablespoons shredded coconut that has been lightly toasted under the broiler (grill).*

# Spanish tortilla

A classic pantry dish, this tastes great cold or hot and in Spain, slices are placed into bread rolls for a light lunch or snack. You can also serve it to friends as a tapa. A cast-iron frying pan is ideal for making this dish.

Preparation 10 minutes
Cooking time 30 minutes

## INGREDIENTS
*Serves 4*

potatoes — 4 medium, (about 14 oz/400 g)
olive oil — ¼ cup
onion — 1, chopped
red pepper (capsicum) — ½, chopped

eggs — 4
salt — ½ tspn
freshly ground black pepper
anchovy fillets — 6, drained

## TO MAKE

1. Peel and dice potatoes into ½ in. (1 cm) cubes. Pat dry with paper towels.
2. Heat oil in in a heavy-based frying pan until smoking. Add potatoes in a single layer and cook slowly over medium heat for about 15 minutes, stirring occasionally — they should become only lightly golden (do not allow them to crisp).
3. When tender, remove from pan and fry onion and pepper in pan until tender, about 3 minutes.
4. Beat eggs with salt and pepper. Combine in a bowl with potatoes, onion, and pepper.
5. There should be about 1 tablespoon of oil left in frying pan. If not, add some more. Heat until smoking then pour in egg mixture. Lay anchovies fillets on top. Cook on low heat until most of the egg has set, about 5 minutes. To cook egg on top, pop pan under broiler (grill), leaving the handle to stick out if it isn't heat proof.

## VARIATIONS:

• *For a classic tortilla espanola, leave out the red pepper and anchovies — purists don't even use the onion. If you can be bothered, slice the potatoes very thinly instead of dicing them. Cook in batches, a single layer at a time, without letting them crisp. The extra effort pays off with improved taste and texture.*
• *You can add almost anything your heart desires: diced chorizo or ham can be fried with the onions. Or you could add some green in the form of peas or shredded rocket (arugula). Freshly chopped parsley or basil can be added to the eggs, as can grated cheese.*
• *The potatoes can also be cooked in stock. Fry them for a few minutes in a couple of tablespoons of olive oil over medium-high heat until golden. Then add a cup of stock and simmer potatoes until tender.*

# Pasta frittata

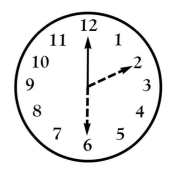

*Since this dish tastes good warm or at room temperature, you can take leftovers to work the next day and it also makes ideal picnic fare. It can be a handy way to use leftover pasta, vegetables, or meat. The frying pan should be about 8-10 inches (20-25 cm) in diameter. If its handle isn't heat-proof, make sure it sticks out from under the broiler (grill).*

Preparation 10 minutes
Cooking time 20 minutes

## INGREDIENTS

*Serves 4*

butter — 1 tbspn
olive oil — 2 tbspns
garlic — 2 cloves, chopped
leek — 1, chopped
bacon — 2 strips (rashers), chopped
eggs — 4, lightly beaten

milk or cream — 2 tbspns
salt and freshly ground black pepper
parmesan — freshly grated, ½ cup
fettuccine — 8 oz (250 g), broken in half and
    cooked until just al dente (see page 4)

## TO MAKE

1. Melt butter with 1 tablespoon olive oil in a heavy-based frying pan. Add garlic, leek, and bacon and cook until leek is soft, about 5 minutes. Remove from pan; set aside.
2. Combine eggs, milk, salt, lots of pepper, and half the parmesan in a large bowl. Mix in cooked pasta.
3. Heat remaining oil over low heat in same pan. Add half the pasta mixture. Top with bacon mixture, then rest of pasta mixture. Using a plate, press down firmly to pack tight. Sprinkle remaining parmesan on top.
4. Cook 12 minutes to brown bottom, then place under hot broiler (grill) to set and brown top.

## VARIATIONS

• *Serve frittata with passata or Italian tomato sauce (see pages 9 and 20) and a green salad.*
• *Try incorporating any chopped vegetables you have on hand — tomato, mushrooms, peppers (capsicum), zucchini (courgette), or rocket (arugula) — instead of, or with, the leek at the start.*
• *Substitute ham, salami, pancetta, or leftover cooked meat for the bacon.*
• *Herbs make a welcome addition, fresh or dried. Try basil, oregano, or thyme.*
• *Add a handful of shredded mozzarella with the parmesan if you like it cheesier. This will also help it to hold together.*

# Onion and cheese flan

The frozen pastry now available is good quality and only takes minutes to thaw so it is perfect for afterwork meals. You can make individual flans (or quiches or tarts, whatever you choose to call them) using small pans if you prefer but cooking a larger tart makes a lot of sense as you can eat it cold the next day. You don't have to use a quiche dish or pie pan — a shallow, rectangular baking dish will work too but you may have to increase the quantities.
If you use more than a single sheet of pastry, brush the edge of one with water, overlap it by about ½ in. (1 cm) with the other sheet and press down firmly to join.

Preparation 2-5 minutes
Cooking time 30 minutes

## INGREDIENTS

*Serves 4*
butter — 2 tbspns
water — ¼ cup
salt — ½ tspn
onions — thinly sliced, 1½ cups

frozen shortcrust pastry — 1 sheet, thawed
eggs — 3, lightly beaten
milk — ½ cup
cheese —grated, ½ cup

## TO MAKE

1. Preheat oven to 375°F (190°C/Gas 5).
2. Melt butter with water and salt in saucepan. Add onions, cover tightly, and cook over low heat until onion is soft. Drain.
3. Meanwhile, line a lightly greased pan with pastry.
4. Combine eggs, milk, and cheese. Add onions, mix well, and pour into pastry case.
5. Bake about 25 minutes, or until a knife inserted in the middle comes out clean.
6. Let stand for 5 minutes if serving hot. Can also be served cold.

## VARIATIONS

• *Use cream or half milk/half cream for a richer filling. Or just the yolk of the third egg.*
• *The cheese you use will affect the taste. Swiss or gruyere work well.*
• *Use leeks instead of onions in exactly the same way. Add some bacon at the same time if desired.*
• *Lay slices of tomato, black olives, and anchovy fillets on top of the filling before baking. Spinach works well with this combination — steam it first (see page 44).*
• *Add a few tablespoons of grated parmesan cheese and a few chopped basil leaves to the egg mixture. Lay tomato slices on top and additional slices of gruyere.*
• *Chopped fresh herbs always work — try oregano or thyme.*

# Spiced lentils

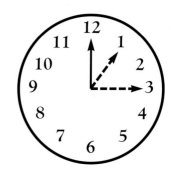

The aioli turns this simple dish into something quite different. This is enough for two people by itself, or the same quantity served with white rice and topped with yogurt instead of aioli will feed four. It's a great side dish, particularly with grilled or baked meat, sausages, or vegetables. If using dried lentils (see page 7) you may wish to add some of the dry spices to the cooking water.

Preparation 5 minutes
Cooking time 10 minutes

## INGREDIENTS

*Serves 2-4*

vegetable oil — 3 tbspns
garlic — 1 clove, chopped
onion — 1, chopped
cumin — 1 tspn
turmeric — ¼ tspn
coriander — 1 tspn
cayenne pepper — ¼ tspn, or to taste

tomato — 3 large, or 14 oz (440 g) can, chopped
ginger — minced, 1 tspn
lentils — 2 x 13 oz (400 g) cans (about 4 cups), undrained
lemon juice — a squeeze (optional)
aioli — to serve (see page 14)

## TO MAKE

1. Place oil, garlic, and onion in a saucepan and cook over low heat until onion is soft.
2. Add spices and stir 1 minute.
3. Add tomato and ginger and cook until tomato is soft.

4. Add lentils and lemon juice and heat through. If possible, let stand for a few minutes to allow the lentils to absorb the spices.
5. Serve with a dollop of aioli.

# Salad nicoise

*This classic salad is given new life with a few contemporary variations. You can also make a good pantry-only salad by mixing the tuna and dressing with a sliced onion (preferably purple/spanish), 2 cloves of crushed garlic, and a 13 oz (400 g) can of cannellini or white haricot beans — refrigerate for as long as possible then serve with toasted bread.*

**Preparation 5 minutes**
**Cooking time 20 minutes**

## INGREDIENTS

*Serves 4*

potatoes — 10 whole baby (new) or 5 large, cut in quarters
frozen broad ( fava) beans — 7 oz (200 g )
tomatoes — 4, cut into wedges
tuna — 2 x 7 oz (200 g) cans, drained and flaked with a fork
anchovy fillets — 4
black olives — ½ cup
eggs — 4, hard-cooked (boiled)

*DRESSING*

white wine vinegar — 1 tbspn
extra virgin olive oil — 6 tbspns
lemon — juice of 1
salt — big pinch

## TO MAKE

1. Boil potatoes until tender, about 15-20 minutes; drain and cool slightly.
2. Meanwhile, cook beans until tender; drain and cool slightly.
3. Place potatoes and beans in a bowl with tomatoes and tuna.
5. Mix dressing ingredients. Pour desired amount over salad and toss lightly.
6. Top with anchovies, olives, and eggs. Serve while still slightly warm or at room temperature.

## VARIATIONS

• *Use roma (plum) tomatoes if possible, cut into thick slices*
• *Cooking the tomatoes is a non-traditional quirk that will lift this dish immeasurably. Halve them, then roast (see page 44) and cool.*
• *Add strips of roasted red pepper (capsicum) (see page 42) for a lively difference.*
• *Use fresh green beans instead of frozen broad beans.*
• *Use chunks of seared fresh tuna steak instead of canned tuna.*
• *Add extra bulk with salad greens.*
• *Aoili (see page 14) can be substituted for the vinaigrette dressing.*

# Beans with sage and tomato

*Serving size depends on the bread or pasta used — short pasta such as pennette is recommended. Choose broad or fava, cannellini, small haricot, or white beans. This is also a wonderful side dish to grilled or broiled meat such as sausages or chicken breast, or as part of an antipasto plate.*

**Preparation 5 minutes**
**Cooking time 15 minutes**

## INGREDIENTS

*Serves 2-4*

olive oil — 3 tbspns
garlic — 2 cloves, finely chopped
bacon — 2 strips (rashers), chopped
sweet paprika — 1 tbspn
sage — 4-6 leaves, chopped

tomatoes — 2 large or 13 oz (400 g) can (drained), chopped
beans — 2 x 13 oz (400 g) cans
salt and freshly ground pepper
toasted bread or hot pasta — to serve

## TO MAKE

1. Place oil, garlic, and bacon in a saucepan and sauté until bacon is just starting to cook.
2. Add paprika, sage, and tomatoes and cook until tomatoes are soft.
3. Add beans and gently heat through for 5-10 minutes to allow the beans to absorb the flavors.
5. Season with salt and pepper. Serve hot with bread or pasta.

## VARIATIONS

• *You can use ground sage, to taste, instead of fresh but it won't be as flavorsome.*
• *Pancetta can be used instead of bacon, or try a spicier meat such as chorizo.*
• *Dried beans can be used but you will have to soak them overnight (see page 7).*
• *You can also serve this dish at room temperature with fresh bread or as part of an antipasto plate.*

# Cream of spinach soup

This is a great "from-the-pantry" dish as the only fresh ingredient is the cream, and frozen chopped spinach works far better for this recipe than fresh. You can use packs of chicken stock or frozen home-made stock.

**Preparation 2 minutes**
**Cooking time 20 minutes**

## INGREDIENTS

*Serves 4*

frozen spinach — 3 packs
    (about 1½ lb/750 g), chopped
butter or olive oil — 2 tbspns
onion — 1 small, finely chopped
garlic — 1 clove, finely chopped
all-purpose (plain) flour — 2 tbspns

chicken stock — 4 cups
salt and pepper — to taste
nutmeg — ½ tspn, or to taste
light whipping cream — 1 cup
cayenne pepper or hot pepper sauce
    — to taste

## TO MAKE

1. Place unthawed spinach in a saucepan, cover, and cook gently for 10 minutes or until softened. Drain well and transfer to a food processor.
2. Place butter in saucepan and cook onion and garlic until onion is soft.
3. Sprinkle in flour, and stir until onion is golden.
4. Add stock and boil 5 minutes, stirring.
5. Add half this liquid to spinach in food processor and puree until smooth. Return to the saucepan and season with salt, pepper, and nutmeg.
6. Add cream and heat gently — do not boil.
7. Serve with sprinkle of cayenne or a dash of hot pepper sauce.

## VARIATIONS

• *Smoked salmon, chopped or cut into thin strips, can be scattered on top.*
• *If you prefer something more flavorsome, try adding spices with the onion: 1 teaspoon ground cumin, 2 teaspoons mustard seeds, 2 teaspoons chopped ginger, 1 chopped garlic clove, 1 chopped red chili.*
• *Experiment with the taste of fenugreek, cloves, and cinnamon — ¼ teaspoon of any of these is a place to start.*

# Tomato and coconut soup

*Another dish that puts pantry ingredients to clever use. This makes a delicious difference from canned tomato soup as a light meal, and is good enough to serve to guests as a first course if you are caught unaware. Pureeing the tomatoes makes the soup almost frothy.*

Preparation 2 minutes
Cooking time 10 minutes

## INGREDIENTS

*Serves 2-4*

tomatoes — 2 x 14 oz (440 g) cans,
    with juice
sugar — 2 tspns
salt — 1 tspn
plain (all-purpose) flour — 2 tbspn
vegetable oil — 1 tbspn

ground coriander — 2 tspns
cumin — 2 tspns
cayenne pepper or chili powder —
    ½ tspn or to taste
coconut cream (thick) — 1 cup
black pepper — freshly ground

## TO MAKE

1. Puree tomatoes with sugar, salt, and flour in a food processor.
2. Heat oil in saucepan and cook spices until fragrant, about 1 minute.
3. Add coconut cream and pureed tomatoes. Simmer, stirring, for a few minutes until slightly thickened. Season with pepper to taste.

## VARIATIONS

• *Serve sprinkled with chopped cilantro (fresh coriander leaves) or basil.*
• *Instead of the spices, use 1 teaspoon each crushed garlic and ginger. Then, add a tablespoon of chili sauce and a dash of teriyaki sauce with the coconut cream.*
• *For a curried corn and tomato soup, follow the basic recipe but instead of the spices use 1 teaspoon crushed garlic, 2 teaspoons curry powder, and 1 small onion, chopped. Then add a 5 oz/150 g can of corn kernels with the coconut cream.*
• *You can use 1 oz (30 g) creamed coconut dissolved in 1 cup water instead of the coconut cream.*

# Clam chowder

This soup is big on comfort value, small on effort. You can make up the total quantity of liquid in this recipe (4 cups) with a combination of clam juice, milk, cream, water, and stock, depending on what you have available. If using mainly milk, you may need to add some with water in Step 5 to provide enough liquid for the potatoes, but keep the heat low when cooking. Fish stock can be purchased in packs and stored in the cupboard. No need to remove fat from bacon as no extra fat is added for cooking in this dish.

Preparation 5 minutes
Cooking time 25 minutes

## INGREDIENTS

*Serves 2-4*

clams — 14 oz (440 g) can, undrained
bacon — 2 rashers, chopped
onion — 1 small, chopped
potatoes — 3 large, peeled and diced
    (about 3 cups)

salt and white pepper
fish stock or water— 1½ cups
light whipping cream — ½ cup
milk — ½ cup

## TO MAKE

1. Remove clams from liquid; reserving 1½ cups liquid. Chop into small chunks.
2. Fry bacon in saucepan over low heat until crisp.
3. Add onion and saute over medium heat until soft.
4. Add potatoes and toss through.
5. Add salt and pepper, reserved liquid, and stock. Simmer 15 minutes until potatoes are tender.
6.  Add clams, cream and milk, and gently heat through. Let stand if possible (see note). Reheat if necessary and serve warm.

## VARIATIONS

• *Chowder improves with standing so, if you have time, let stand off the heat for 1 hour or refrigerate overnight before reheating.*
• *Serve topped with fresh chopped chives or thyme and freshly ground black pepper.*
• *Salted crackers are the traditional accompaniment.*
• *You may like to add a handful of finely chopped celery, green pepper (capsicum), and/or carrot with the potatoes.*
• *Corn chowder can be made by using canned corn kernels instead of clams, and vegetable or chicken stock instead of fish stock.*

# Simple onion soup

*This may take more than a few minutes to cook but the beauty of this recipe is that you don't have to do anything in that time (except relax on the couch or clean the bathroom). It's also one of those "something from almost nothing" dishes that you can happily serve at a dinner party as a first course. Even the bread can be stale.*

Preparation 5 minutes
Cooking time 50 minutes

## INGREDIENTS

*Serves 4-6*
butter — 3 tbspns
onions — 1 lb (500 g), thinly sliced
dry white wine — 1 cup
water — 1/2 cup
beef or chicken stock — 5 cups

salt and freshly ground black pepper
baguette (French breadstick) —
    sliced and toasted
gruyere cheese — freshly grated

## TO MAKE

1. Melt butter in deep, heavy-bottomed pan. Add onions, wine, and water and cook very gently on low heat until onions are soft, about 30-40 minutes, stirring regularly.
2. Add stock and season to taste. Bring to boil, cover, and simmer 10 minutes.
3. Meanwhile, top toasted bread with grated cheese and broil (grill) until cheese is melted and golden.
4. Divide soup amongst individual bowls, top each with a slice or two of bread. Serve immediately.

## VARIATIONS

• *If you love cheese, you may like to add loads of gruyere and maybe a bit of parmesan on top.*
• *You can also place unmelted cheese and toast on top of the individual soup bowls and then pop the whole lot under the broiler (grill) so that the entire top is covered with cheese.*

# Easy-to-make laksa

Laksa is a one-bowl meal of noodles in a curried coconut broth that can be found in various forms across south-east Asia. Traditionally, it contains all sorts of exotic ingredients like ground candlenuts which do add up to a perfect laksa. This afterwork version still hits the spot, but there's a warning — this dish is addictive!

Preparation 2 minutes
Cooking time 35 minutes

## INGREDIENTS

*Serves 4*

minced chili (sambal olek) — ½-1 tbspn
minced garlic — 1 tspn
minced ginger — 1 tspn
ground coriander — 1 tspn
turmeric — 1 tspn
palm sugar or brown sugar — ½ tspn
lemongrass — 1 in. (2.5 cm) piece, chopped, or zest of ½ lemon (optional)
fish sauce (nam pla) — 2 tspns, or 1 tspn shrimp paste

peanut oil — 1 tbspn
chicken stock — 6 cups (full-strength)
Chinese egg noodles — 4 oz (125 g)
coconut milk — 14 fl oz (440 ml) can
bean sprouts — 7 oz (220 g), fresh or canned
scallions (spring onions/shallots) — 6, chopped

## TO MAKE

1. Mix together chili, garlic, ginger, coriander, turmeric, sugar, lemongrass, and fish sauce in a small bowl to form a paste.
2. Heat oil into a large saucepan over medium heat. Add paste and cook until fragrant, about 2 minutes.
3. Add stock and simmer 15 minutes.
4. Add coconut milk and simmer gently for another 10 minutes.
5. Meanwhile, prepare noodles as directed on packet. Drain.
6. Add noodles, bean sprouts, and scallions to laksa and leave on low heat for a few more minutes to allow flavors to mingle. Serve hot.

## VARIATIONS

• *Top with chopped fresh mint and more chili if desired.*
• *Add 7 oz (200 g) chicken fillet. Cut into strips and stir-fry in peanut oil, then remove and cook spices. Return chicken to pan with stock.*
• *Add 8 oz (250 g) fresh shelled prawns with the stock. Use fish stock, instead of chicken stock: you can use commercial stock or make one by simmering prawn heads and shells in water for 20 minutes.*
• *Add cubes of tofu with coconut milk.*
• *Try a combination of chicken, prawns, and tofu.*

# Peasant bean soup

There are endless variations around this theme, not the least being the vegetables that can be added along with the onion — diced carrots, shredded cabbage, sliced zucchini (courgettes), broccoli, and the like. It is best to use either long threads of pasta like spaghetti, broken into pieces, or small shapes like elbow macaroni.

Preparation 5 minutes
Cooking time 25 minutes

## INGREDIENTS

*Serves 4*
olive oil — 1 tbspn
garlic — 2 cloves, chopped
brown onion — 1 large, chopped
peeled tomatoes — 14 oz (440 g) can, undrained
borlotti beans — 13 oz (400 g) can

chicken stock — 4 cups
tomato paste — 1/4 cup
thyme — 1 tspn dried or 2 tspns fresh
basil — 1 tspn dried or 1 tbspns fresh
bay leaf — 1
pasta — 4 oz (125g)

## TO MAKE

1. Place oil, garlic, and onion in deep, heavy-bottomed saucepan and cook over medium heat until onion is soft.
2. Add tomatoes with juice, break up roughly, and cook for a couple of minutes.
3. Add beans, stock, tomato paste and herbs and simmer gently 10 minutes.
4. Add pasta and simmer until soft, about 5-10 minutes.

## VARIATIONS

• *Serve with freshly grated parmesan.*
• *Substitute any kind of bean: red kidney, cannellini, black-eyed peas, even a can of mixed beans.*
• *If you don't have stock, use 2 undrained cans peeled tomatoes and 1/2 cup water.*
• *Try a sliced leek instead of the onion.*
• *Use 1/2 teaspoon ground coriander instead of thyme, and add 1 teaspoon chili powder (or to taste).*
• *Add chopped bacon with the onions.*
• *Add 1 cup roughly chopped fresh spinach or curly endive.*
• *Instead of beans and pasta, mash 1 large potato and stir it through the soup. Throw in a handful of black olives.*
• *Or replace beans and pasta with a cup each of lentils and uncooked rice, and cook for 20-30 minutes.*

# Simple Italian broths

These recipes are a perfect illustration of how simplicity can be perfection. The best results will come from using the finest quality ingredients — good home-made stock from the freezer and the indispensible wedge of parmesan — and a gentle approach to sautéeing vegetables. If using store-bought stock, which is usually much more concentrated, make up the 6 cups with half stock, half water as only a light broth is required. The egg and parmesan soup is an Italian dish known as strachiatelli. The zucchini recipe works incredibly well using oyster mushrooms as a substitute.

Preparation 2-5 minutes
Cooking time 5-30 minutes

## Egg and parmesan

### INGREDIENTS
*Serves 4*

chicken stock — 6 cups
eggs — 3
parmesan — freshly grated, 2 tbspns
parsley — chopped, 1 tbspn
salt and freshly ground black pepper

### TO MAKE

1. Bring stock to boil in a saucepan.
2. Whisk eggs until frothy. Add parmesan, parsley, and seasonings.
3. When stock is at a rolling boil (bubbling very fast), pour in egg, whisking constantly with a fork until the egg sets in long strands.
4. Serve immediately.

## Zucchini broth

### INGREDIENTS
*Serves 4*

olive oil — 1 tbspn
garlic — 2 cloves, crushed
onion — 2 white, thinly sliced
zucchini (courgette)— 4 large,
    very thinly sliced
chicken stock — 6 cups
pinch salt
black pepper — freshly ground
parmesan — freshly grated, to serve

### TO MAKE

1. Place olive oil and garlic in a saucepan over low heat and cook until garlic is fragrant. Add onions, stir, and cook for a few minutes until they soften.
2. Stir in zucchini and cook for 5-10 minutes until zucchini softens.
3. Add a third of the stock and simmer gently for 5 minutes.
4. Add salt, pepper, and remaining stock, and simmer for another 5-10 minutes so that zucchini is very soft but not falling apart.
5. Serve with freshly grated parmesan sprinkled on top.

# Chinese noodle soup

When the kitchen seems bare, your energy levels are at an absolute minimum, and your main concern is to feed yourself something fast, rely on a quick Asian soup. This is a good way of using up leftover chicken if you have it, or quickly pan-fry a chicken fillet. Fresh Chinese egg noodles can be bought in packs (and need only 30 seconds in boiling water) or dry (which need boiling for a few minutes to cook). This soup needs only a light broth so use either frozen home-made stock or dilute commercial stock (which is usually quite concentrated) so that it is half stock, half water. Depending on the stock and soy sauce you use, you may wish to adjust the salt which is an integral part of Chinese soups.

*Preparation 2 minutes*
*Cooking time 5 minutes*

## INGREDIENTS

*Serves 1*

chicken stock — 3 cups (total when diluted)
Chinese egg noodles — 2 oz (60 g), cooked
soy sauce — 1-2 tbspn
oyster sauce — 1 tspn
salt — to taste
dry sherry — 1/2-1 tbspn (optional)
chicken — 1 cup, cooked and shredded

## TO MAKE

1. Heat stock in a saucepan.
2. If using dry noodles, boil them in stock for a few minutes according to packet directions.
3. Add sauces, salt, and sherry. Taste and adjust seasonings.
4. Place shredded chicken in a bowl.
5. Pour stock and noodles over and serve hot.

## VARIATIONS

• *This soup definitely benefits from a generous amount of chili, either chopped fresh, minced from the jar, or as chili sauce or paste.*
• *Add 1/4 teaspoon or more freshly grated ginger.*
• *Add a dash of sesame oil.*
• *Top with chopped scallions (spring onions/ shallots) and cilantro (coriander leaves).*
• *Add 1/4 cup chopped ham with chicken.*
• *Add some Chinese greens (cabbage or bok choy, for example) or steamed broccoli to broth while heating.*
• *Rice noodles can be used instead of egg noodles, if you prefer.*

# Marinated tomatoes

This dish focuses on tomatoes, which, in season, are inexpensive, plentiful, and taste divine. Try the same ingredients prepared in a number of ways, and serve as a light summer meal, a side dish, or an appetizer. If you can, let the tomatoes stand for the full hour to allow flavors to mingle.

*Preparation 10-60 minutes*

## INGREDIENTS

*Serves 2-4*
basil leaves — 8, chopped
garlic — 1 clove, finely chopped
extra virgin olive oil — 4 tbspns

ripe red tomatoes — 8, chopped roughly
ricotta cheese — 2 cups
bread, pita bread, or pasta — to serve

## TO MAKE

1. Combine basil, garlic, and oil.
2. Pour over tomatoes and let stand for up to 1 hour (10 minutes will do).
3. Pile ricotta on top and serve at room temperature with the accompaniment of your choice.

## VARIATIONS

• *You can eat the tomatoes with slices of dense bread or torn pieces of pita bread, toasted under the broiler (grill).*
• *Try tossing tomato and ricotta (still at room temperature) through hot pasta.*
• *If serving as a salad with bread, you could add 2 teaspoons balsamic or red wine vinegar to the oil mixture if desired.*
• *Leave out the ricotta and pile the tomatoes on top of toasted Italian bread — you have the beloved Italian dish, bruschetta.*
• *If you can be bothered, this will taste even better if you skin the tomatoes. Make a cross with a knife at the bottom end and then place them in a bowl of extremely hot water for 5 minutes. Remove, allow to cool a little, then peel of the skins.*
• *Cottage cheese can provide a handy substitute for ricotta.*

# Thai beef salad

This refreshing salad is served at room temperature and makes a light summer meal on its own, or serve it as a first course when entertaining or as part of an Asian selection, perhaps with a red or green curry (see page 8) and spicy peanut noodles (see page 52).

**Preparation 10 minutes**
**Cooking 5 minutes**

## INGREDIENTS

*Serves 2-4*
sirloin (boneless rump) steak — 1½ lb (750 g)
lettuce, preferably cos — ½
Spanish (purple) onion — 1 large
continental (Lebanese) cucumber — 1 small
fresh basil or mint — chopped, 2-4 tbspns
cilantro (fresh coriander leaves) —
     chopped, 2-4 tbspns

## TO MAKE

1. Sear steak in a hot frying pan or under broiler (grill) for a few minutes each side until cooked; try to leave it pink in the middle.
2. Meanwhile, combine dressing ingrdients and set aside.
3. Remove meat from heat and let rest by placing it on a cool surface (such as a plate or chopping board).
4. Prepare salad ingredients: tear lettuce into pieces, cut onion into thin wedges, slice cucumber into thin strips. Place in large bowl.
5. Add basil and cilantro to dressing and pour over salad.
6. Slice meat into very thin strips. Add to salad, toss, and serve.

## DRESSING

lime juice — 4 tbspns
fish sauce (nam pla) — 4 tbspns
chilis — 2, seeded and finely chopped
garlic — 1 clove, finely chopped
ginger — about 1 in. (2 cm) piece, peeled
     and grated
palm sugar or brown sugar — 1 tspn

## VARIATIONS

• *You can stir-fry steak in a little sesame oil in a wok if preferred.*
• *Slices of scallion (spring onion/shallots) or white onion can be substituted for Spanish onion.*
• *Remember the jar of minced chili if whole fresh chilis aren't available.*

# Spinach salad with walnuts

*This light salad with a mild, nutty flavor is good served with cold cured meats such as pastrami, ham, prosciutto, or rare roast beef and hard-cooked (boiled) eggs chopped in half. Bocconcini is a very mild Italian cheese that comes in white balls which you'll find in your deli stored in jars of liquid. Experiment with other cheeses and ingredients such as those suggested below.*

Preparation 5 minutes

## INGREDIENTS

*Serves 2-4*
walnut halves — ⅔ cup
English spinach — 1 bunch
bocconcini cheese — 4, sliced or quartered
black pepper — cracked

## TO MAKE

1. Toast walnut halves on a baking tray under a hot broiler (grill).
2. Cut off tough part of stems from spinach and arrange leaves in salad bowl.
3. Add bocconcini, walnuts, and pepper.
4. Mix dressing ingredients, pour desired quantity over the salad, and toss lightly.

## DRESSING

walnut oil blended to taste with peanut oil — 5 tbspns total
red wine or rasberry vinegar — 1 tbspn
lemon juice — a squeeze

## VARIATIONS

• *Blue cheese always works well with spinach and walnuts, so you could crumble some into the salad instead of bocconcini or make it into a dressing by blending to taste with a few tablespoons of olive oil, lemon juice, and either crème fraîche or sour cream.*
• *Try chunks of camembert or brie, or shavings of parmesan instead of bocconcini.*
• *Crisp cook slices of prosciutto or bacon under the broiler (grill) and add to the salad.*
• *Toss in very thin strips of red pepper (capsicum) — roasted first if you like.*
• *Add caramellized Spanish (purple) onion. Cut it, unpeeled, into thick slices then cook under a hot broiler (grill) until very brown, brushing regularly with olive oil. Cool and peel before tossing into salad.*
• *Substitute other salad leaves such as rocket (arugula).*

# Baked vegetables Mediterranean-style

An absolutely no-fuss method of cooking vegetables that can then be served in a myriad of ways. You will want to enjoy the pan juices so don't be frugal with the olive oil — soak it up with crusty bread.

**Preparation 10 minutes**
**Cooking time 30-60 minutes**

## INGREDIENTS

*Serves 4*

eggplant (aubergine) — 1 large, or
    8 baby ones
zucchinis (courgette)— 4, halved lengthwise
salt
red peppers (capsicum) — 2, halved
    and seeded
leeks — 2, halved lengthwise

plum (roma) tomatoes — 2, halved,
    or ½ punnet of cherry tomatoes
black olives — 1 cup
extra virgin olive oil — ½ cup
garlic — 4 cloves, chopped
freshly ground black pepper
crusty white bread — to serve

## TO MAKE

1. Preheat oven to 475°F (240°C/Gas 9).
2. If using large eggplant, cut into slices about ½ in. (1 cm) thick, or cut baby eggplant in half lengthwise. Sprinkle this and zucchini with salt and let stand 10 minutes or longer for juices to disgorge, then pat dry with paper towels. Meanwhile, prepare other vegetables as directed.
3. Place vegetables in large baking dish and drizzle with olive oil (you may like to brush to ensure they are well-coated). Sprinkle with garlic, salt, and pepper.
3. Bake on highest shelf for about 30-60 minutes, regularly basting or brushing with olive oil. The vegetables will soften and caramellize, turning dark brown on the edges. If different vegetables are cooking unevenly, remove cooked ones from oven and return near the end to warm through.
4. If desired, warm bread in the oven on a separate shelf in the last few minutes.

## VARIATIONS

• *Other vegetables that work well include: halved bulbs of fennel, whole baby squash, peeled onions (either whole or quartered), large flat mushroom caps. Smaller vegetable pieces may need to be added later in the cooking time.*
• *Sprinkle with fresh rosemary or chopped basil or dried oregano leaves before roasting. For more middle eastern flavors, try ground cumin and cayenne pepper.*
• *You can roast whole unpeeled cloves of garlic or an entire head along with the vegetables (see page 9).*
• *Crumble 3 oz (90 g) goats cheese (chevre) or feta on top when serving.*
• *Cut cooked vegetables into chunks and toss through pasta with goat cheese or parmesan shavings.*
• *Serve hot or cold with couscous.*
• *Toss hot or at room temperature through mixed salad greens and dress with 1 tablespoon balsamic or red wine vinegar.*

# Green vegetable pie

Frozen pastry is an afterwork dream. It's used here to top a "loose" pie without a pastry base. Don't be surprised by the honey in the dish; its sweetness works well with the slightly bitter silverbeet (don't use English spinach). A hint: if you keep your honey jar in the refrigerator, remove lid and heat in the microwave for 10-20 seconds to make the honey runny.

*Preparation about 30 minutes*
*(including thawing)*
*Cooking time 30 minutes*

## INGREDIENTS

*Serves 4*

silverbeet (Swiss chard) — 1 bunch
broccoli — ½ head, broken into florets
zucchini (courgettes) — 2, thinly sliced
eggs — 2, lightly beaten

clear honey — 3 tbspns
filo (phyllo) pastry — 6 sheets, thawed
butter — 3 tbspns, melted
cheddar cheese — grated, 2 cups

## TO MAKE

1. Preheat oven to 350°F (180°C/Gas 4).
2. Roughly tear the silverbeet and wash and drain well.
3. Place all vegetables, eggs, and honey in a large bowl and toss well to combine.
4. Pack mixture tightly into shallow baking dish (about 10 x 8 in./25 x 20 cm).

Cover with 2 sheets of pastry, tucking in the sides, and brush with butter. Continue to layer pastry on top, two sheets at a time, brushing each layer with butter.
5. Bake 30 minutes or until pastry is golden brown. Let rest a few minutes. Serve hot or cold.

# Salmon with green vegetables

The variations on this recipe may read like completely different dishes, and they are. They do, however, share a common theme. Salmon, of any kind, goes well with green vegetables and the comfortable contrasting texture of pine nuts. Just remember to keep the mustard flavor gentle as well — no hot English mustard here, or even robust grainy mustard. Choose the milder Dijon varieties.

Preparation 10 minutes

## INGREDIENTS

*Serves 2 as a main*
3 oz (90 g) smoked salmon,
    cut into thin strips
asparagus spears — 8, blanched in
    boiling water until tender crisp
cos lettuce, butter lettuce, or baby spinach
pine nuts — 1/2 cup, toasted

## METHOD

1. Place salad ingredients in a bowl.
2. Mix together dressing ingredients and pour over salad.
3. Toss well and serve immediately.

## DRESSING

whole-egg mayonnaise or crème fraîche
    — 4 tbspns
chives — chopped, 2 tbspns (optional)
dijon mustard — 1 tspn or to taste

## VARIATIONS

• *Add slices of avocado to the salad.*
• *Try a salad with pieces of crisp-fried bacon instead of the salmon.*
• *Replace the asparagus with raw strips of cucumber.*
• *Try it as a hot dish. Warm the salmon in a pan with 1 tablespoon of white wine until the wine has almost evaporated. Add the mustard, chives, and crème fraîche and toss through pasta with the pine nuts and blanched asparagus. You could add baby spinach to the salmon in the pan if desired.*
• *Fresh salmon could be used if available. Sear a salmon steak in a pan with a little olive oil for about 3 minutes on each side, then break into pieces. The salmon should be only just cooked.*

# Pizza and open sandwiches

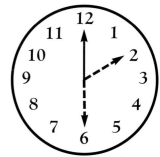

Preparation 5-10 minutes
Cooking time 5-20 minutes

*You can make gourmet pizzas that are quite different from those you can buy. Make them in small sizes to feed one or two, in larger sizes, or make an assortment to feed a crowd. Here are a few suggestions to get you started. The method is fairly standard — layer on the toppings, then pop under the broiler (grill) for a few minutes until the top has heated and the cheese has melted.*

## INGREDIENTS

*FOR THE BASE*

- pre-prepared pizza base (these often need cooking in a moderate oven for about 10-20 minutes after brushing it with oil and covering with toppings)
- pita bread (brushed with oil)
- flour tortilla (brushed with oil and pricked with a fork)
- foccacia bread
- Turkish pidé bread, split open
- squares of frozen puff pastry (thawed, brushed with melted butter, and cooked in a moderate oven after topping according to time on packet)

## TO MAKE

*FOR THE TOP*

- Spread the base with tomato paste and sprinkle with dried oregano. Add slices of salami, green pepper (capsicum), tomato and mushroom, and top with mozzarella.
- Spread the base with Mexican tomato salsa. Add shredded chicken and slices of avocado, and top with cheddar or Monteray jack cheese.
- Spread the base with tomato paste and sprinkle with fresh or dried thyme. Add slices of Spanish (purple) onion, black olives, and fillets of sardines (from the can and drained).

- Spread the base with pesto. Add shaved ham, toasted pine nuts and sundried tomatoes and peppers (capsicums), and top with grated parmesan
- Spread the base with hummus. Add slices of roasted eggplant (aubergine) and top with crumbled goats cheese (chevre).
- Spread the base with tapenade. Cover with caramellized onion (slow-cooked in a frying pan with butter until ultra-soft). Top with slices of tomato and parmesan shavings, or small boiled pieces of sweet potato.

# Spiced chicken

Marinating chicken will add both flavor and moistness. The minimum time for marinating is 15 to 30 minutes (time for you to relax or do other things), although overnight is preferable. Cover the chicken with plastic wrap and marinate in the refrigerator for the best results.

*Preparation 30 minutes*
*Cooking time 10 minutes*

## INGREDIENTS
*Serves 4*

ginger — minced, 2 tspns
garlic — 2 cloves, minced
salt — 1 tspn
ground black pepper — ½ tspn
cumin — 1 tspn
paprika — 1 tspn

ground coriander — 2 tspns
flat-leaf parsley or cilantro (coriander leaves) — chopped, 2 tbspns (optional)
lemon juice — 2 tbspns
oil — 3 tbspns
chicken breasts — 2 whole or 4 halves, skin removed

## TO MAKE

1. Combine spices, juice, and oil to make a paste.
2. Rub into chicken and let stand for as long as possible.
3. Heat broiler, grill, or or cast-iron grill pan and cook chicken for about 5 minutes each side, until cooked through.
4. Serve hot or chilled.

## VARIATIONS

• *Serve with vegetables or salad of your choice. You could even shred the cooked chicken and toss into a salad.*
• *You can cut the meat into bite-sized chunks and thread onto skewers before cooking.*
• *The chicken can also be roasted, although this is best with pieces on the bone or even with a whole chicken. It is a longer process but equally hassle-free. Place in a baking dish and cook in a preheated 350°F (180°C/Gas 4) oven for about 45 minutes.*
• *Use yogurt instead of oil for a creamy, low-fat marinade.*
• *Experiment with different ground spice blends: try adding 1 teaspoon each curry powder, garam masala, and/or minced chili. For a Caribbean variation, use ½ teaspoon allspice, ¼ teaspoon thyme, ½ teaspoon salt, big pinch of cinnamon, 2 crushed garlic cloves, 1 tablespoon soy sauce, 1 tablespoon water, ¼ teaspoon minced ginger and minced chili to taste.*

# Baked parcels

Parcels of food are a handy trick as once the ingredients are in their foil wrapping, you can do something else while they cook — maybe make a salad, pop baby (new) potatoes in the oven as well, or boil some white rice. The other great benefit is that there is minimal washing up!

    The suggestions on the following pages all use white meat — either fish or chicken — as it cooks faster than red, and suits the moist steaming of the parcels. Half chicken breasts are recommended, as are white-fleshed fish fillets. In many cases, vegetables are added to the same envelope, making it a real meal in one. All portions are for 4 people.

**Preparation 5 minutes**
**Cooking time 10-20 minutes**

## TO MAKE

1. Preheat oven to 350°F (180°C/Gas 4).
2. For each parcel, you will need a piece of greased foil, big enough to wrap
3. Divide ingredients equally amongst the four parcels — place meat on the middle of the foil sheet, spread any oils or pastes directly onto meat, layer with other ingredients, sprinkle with chopped herbs, and pour any sauces evenly over parcels.
4. Fold the two longest (opposite) sides of foil so that they meet in the middle. Fold this edge over and over so that it will be tightly sealed. Fold up the other ends of parcel.
5. Place parcel on baking sheet with the folded edges up so that the juices do not run out. Bake in oven. Chicken should take about 20 minutes, and fish about 10 minutes, depending on thickness. Thicker pieces may take longer.

*Pictured: Greek fish parcels*

## Spiced parcels

chicken or fish fillets — 4
*spread with a mixture of*
   yogurt — 4 tbspns
   olive oil — 1 tspn
   lemon juice — 1 tbspn
   ground cumin — 2 tspn
   cayenne pepper — 1 tspn
   turmeric — 1 tspn
   garlic — 2 cloves, crushed
   saffron — 1 tspn threads, soaked in
      1 tbspn hot water for 3 minutes

## Greek fish parcel

fish fillets — 4
*spread with*
   olive oil — 4 tspns
*topped with*
   tomatoes — 2 medium, sliced
*sprinkled with*
   black olives — ½ cup, pitted (stoned)
      and roughly chopped
   parsley — chopped, 2 tbspns
   oregano — 1 tbspn chopped fresh or
      2 tspns dried
   garlic — 2 cloves, crushed
   lemon rind — grated, 4 tspns
   lemon juice — 4 tspns

## Asian fish

fish fillets — 4
*topped with*
   scallions (spring onions/shallots) —
      2, sliced
   snow peas (mange tout) — 20
   bamboo shoots — ½ cup
   mint — chopped, 2 tbspns
*sprinkled with a mixture of*
   soy sauce — 1 tbspn
   mild sweet chili sauce — 2 tbspn
   lime or lemon juice — 1 tbspn
   honey — 1 tbspn

## Fish tahini

fish fillets — 4
*spread with*
   tahini — 4 tbspns
*topped with*
   tomato — 8 slices
   fennel — 1 small bulb, thinly sliced
   baby spinach leaves — shredded, 1 cup
   parsley — chopped, 2 tbspns
*sprinkled with*
   lemon juice — 1 tbspn
   olive oil — 2 tbspns
   salt and pepper — to taste

## Pesto chicken

chicken fillets — 4
*spread with*
    pesto (see page 22) — 4 tbspns
*topped with*
    prosciutto — 4 slices, chopped
    zucchini (courgette) — 4 small, sliced
    mozzarella cheese — grated, 4 tbspns

## Orange chicken parcels

chicken fillets — 4
*spread with a mixture of*
    butter — 4 tspns
    garlic — 2 cloves, crushed
*topped with*
    orange — 8 slices, skinned
    thyme — 2 tbspns chopped fresh or
        4 tspns dried mixed herbs
    olives — ½ cup, pitted (stoned)
*sprinkled with a mixture of*
    honey — 2 tspns
    chicken stock — 4 tbspns
    black pepper — cracked

## Garlic herb parcels

chicken fillets — 4
*spread with a mixture of*
    butter — 4 tspns, softened
    garlic — 2 cloves, crushed
    parsley — chopped, 2 tbspns
    chives — chopped, 2 tbspns
    oregano — chopped, 1 tbspn
    thyme — chopped, 1 tbspn
    sundried tomatoes— chopped, 2 tbspns

## Mediterranean chicken parcels

chicken fillets — 4
*spread with*
    tapenade (see page 9) — 4 tbspns
*topped with*
    red pepper (capsicum) —
        1, cut into strips
    eggplant (aubergine) — 1, thinly sliced
*sprinkled with*
    garlic — 2 cloves, crushed
    thyme — 2 tbspns chopped fresh or
        4 tspns dried
    parmesan — freshly grated, ½ cup
    pine nuts — 2 tbspns, toasted

## Peasant chicken parcels

chicken fillets — 4
*topped with*
    bacon — 4 slices (rashers), chopped
    mushrooms — 4, sliced
    carrot — 1, thinly sliced
    bay leaves — 4
*sprinkled with*
    rosemary — 4 sprigs fresh or
        4 tspns dried
*covered with a mixture of*
    thick cream — 4 tbspns
    pink peppercorns — canned, 2 tbspns
    seeded mustard — 2 tbspns

# Mustard chicken parcels

chicken fillets — 4
*topped with*
    leek — 1 small, finely sliced
*covered with a mixture of*
    dijon mustard — 4 tbspns
    sour cream — 4 tbspns
    chicken stock — 2 tbspns
    garlic — 2 cloves, crushed
    marjoram — 2 tbspns chopped fresh or
      4 tspns dried mixed herbs
*sprinkled after baking with*
    flaked almonds — 2 tbspns, toasted

# Italian chicken parcels

chicken fillets — 4
*spread with*
    tomato puree — 4 tbspns
*topped with*
    zucchini — 3, sliced
    mushrooms — 4-6, sliced
*sprinkled with*
    olive oil — 4 tspns
    baby capers — 4 tbspns
    garlic — 2 cloves, crushed
    basil — 2 tbspns chopped fresh or
      1 tspn dried

# Oriental chicken parcels

chicken fillets — 4, cut into strips
*topped with*
    chinese cabbage — ½, finely shredded
    baby corn — 1 small can, drained
*that has been tossed with*
    ginger — 2 tspns grated
    cilantro (coriander leaves) —
      chopped, 2 tbspns
    oyster sauce — 4 tbspns
*sprinkled with*
    sesame seeds — 1 tbspn

# Green herbed parcels

chicken fillets — 4
*spread with a mixture of*
    crème fraîche — 4 tbspns
    mixed herbs (chives, chevril, dill) —
      2 tbspns chopped fresh
    lemon rind— grated, 1 tbspn
    garlic — 2 cloves, crushed
    black pepper — cracked
*topped with*
    asparagus — 12 spears
    broccoli florets — 12 pieces

*Pictured: Oriental chicken parcels*

# Index

This 1996 edition is published by Crescent Books,
distributed by Random House Value Publishing, Inc.,
40 Engelhard Avenue, Avenel, New Jersey 07001

Random House
New York • Toronto • London • Sydney • Auckland

A CIP catalog record for this book is available
from the Library of Congress

Published in conjunction with Harbour Books,
an imprint of Lansdowne Publishing Pty Ltd
Level 5, 70 George Street, Sydney, NSW 2000, Australia

Photographer: Rowan Fotheringham
Food Stylist: Suzie Smith
Set in Goudy on Quark Xpress
Printed in Singapore by Tien Wah Press (Pte) Ltd

ISBN 0-517-14247-3

8 7 6 5 4 3 2 1